# DEMOCRACY, PARLIAMENT AND ELECTORAL SYSTEMS

# COMMONWEALTH PARLIAMENTARY ASSOCIATION

The CPA is an association of Commonwealth parliaments and legislatures whose Members, irrespective of gender, race, religion or culture, are united by community of interest, respect for the rule of law and human rights and freedoms, and the pursuit of the positive ideals of parliamentary democracy.

The Association mobilises this diverse grouping of 16 000 Members of approximately 175 national, state, provincial and territorial assemblies into a Commonwealth parliamentary community which shares its experiences and expertise to enhance the governance not just of its own people but of all nations. By fostering improved understanding of both the democratic process and of policies and legislation in other jurisdictions, the Association promotes the continuing advancement of constitutional structures, parliamentary practices and procedures, and policy formulation. It also contributes to the professional development of Parliamentarians and parliamentary staff.

The CPA brings Parliamentarians together through an extensive annual programme of conferences, seminars, workshops, study groups, inter-parliamentary exchanges, and publications and information services. Included in this programme is the publication of books such as this that enable parliamentary practitioners to contribute to the published body of knowledge in the field of representative governance and political theory.

Founded in 1911, the CPA is based in London and has a network of branches in fifty-two of the fifty-four nations of the Commonwealth.

Also available:

*The Overseers: Public Accounts Committees and Public Spending*
David G. McGee, QC

*Women, Public Life and Democracy: Changing Commonwealth*
    *Parliamentary Perspectives*
Compiled and edited by Joni Lovenduski and Rosie Campbell
    with Jacqui Sampson-Jacent

# Democracy, Parliament and Electoral Systems

Edited by
M. A. GRIFFITH-TRAVERSY

Commonwealth Parliamentary Association
in Association with
Pluto Press
London · Sterling, Virginia

First published 2002 by Pluto Press
345 Archway Road, London N6 5AA
and 22883 Quicksilver Drive, Sterling, VA 20166-2012, USA

www.plutobooks.com

British Library Cataloguing in Publication Data
A catalogue record for this book is available from the British Library.

Library of Congress Cataloging-in-Publication Data
A catalog record for this book has been requested.

ISBN 0 7453 2154 2 hardback

Designed and produced for Pluto Press by
Curran Publishing Services, Norwich

Printed and bound in the European Union by
Antony Rowe Ltd, Chippenham and Eastbourne, England

# Contents

**PART IV  COUNTRY-BASED INSIGHTS ON ELECTORAL ISSUES**

**Appendices:**

# Foreword

Since 1994 a productive collaboration between the Commonwealth Parliamentary Association and Wilton Park, an independent agency funded by the UK Foreign and Commonwealth Office, has brought together over 60 delegates each year for discussions on current issues affecting the practice of parliamentary democracy. Parliamentarians nominated by the CPA from the parliaments and legislatures of the Commonwealth have mingled and exchanged views with senior government officials, academics and representatives from international organisations, most of whom come from outside the Commonwealth, in an atmosphere that stimulates and promotes a productive learning process.

Recognising that the beneficial outputs should, so far as possible, be shared with its members who could not participate directly, the CPA has endeavoured to produce a comprehensive report, in the form of a book, on these conferences.

In 2001 the subject chosen for the conference was Parliament, Democracy and Electoral Systems. The broad range of issues covered allowed for discussion on most areas of interest to those involved in politics and public affairs.

The CPA was fortunate to be able to engage the services of Mary Anne Griffith-Traversy, former Deputy Clerk of the House of Commons of Canada, to act as rapporteur. She has produced the enclosed volume which not only captures the views expressed by conference participants, but which also especially reflects her own valuable insights based on many years of parliamentary experience. I extend my sincere gratitude to her.

As my nine-year tenure with the CPA comes to a close I look back on the institution of our CPA/Wilton Park conferences as one of my main legacies to the Association. It would not have happened without a fortuitous meeting in 1993 with Nick Hopkinson, Deputy Director of Wilton Park, whose input to the success of these annual events has been invaluable. I take this opportunity to extend grateful thanks to him.

My colleagues at the CPA Headquarters, particularly Raja Gomez, Director of Development and Planning, have also played important roles in planning and organising the conferences, and I thank him and them.

For ninety years the CPA has been involved in the pursuit of the positive ideals of parliamentary democracy. Over this time thousands of Parliamentarians and parliamentary staff members have made contributions which enable the CPA to further its aims. I commend this book to those interested in continuing this constantly changing, never-ending, and increasingly important work.

Arthur R. Donahoe, QC
Secretary-General
Commonwealth Parliamentary Association
1992–2001

# Preface

For one week in June of 2001, over sixty delegates representing more than thirty countries from all over the world met at Wiston House in the English countryside to discuss parliament, democracy and electoral systems.

The group was composed of politicians and political practitioners, academics and scholars, senators and members, parliamentary speakers, former speakers and prime ministers, heads of international organisations, senior government officials, experts in the structure and functioning of democratic governments from both the practical and the theoretical perspective.

This expert group had been brought together under the joint auspices of the Commonwealth Parliamentary Association (CPA) and Wilton Park, and this event marked the seventh such joint forum.

The prepared papers were wide-ranging and provocative, the presentations diverse and reasoned, the discussions intense and stimulating. All who attended were enriched by the opportunity to learn from others, to share knowledge and experience, to discuss freely and frankly topics and ideas that were of such import, not only for themselves in their ongoing work, but to their countries as well.

It was a great honour for me to have been asked by Mr Arthur R. Donahoe, QC, Secretary-General of the CPA, to participate in these sessions and to prepare a book based upon the papers developed for the conference and the presentations and discussions that took place. It is my hope that I have managed to capture even some of the excitement of those sessions, in order that others may share in the wisdom and rich insights of such a knowledgeable assembly.

Over the course of my many years working in the Canadian House of Commons, the last ten before my retirement as Deputy Clerk, I became very familiar with and deeply impressed by the CPA and the vital role it plays in nurturing and assisting democratic government in Commonwealth countries throughout the world. Under the leadership of Mr Donahoe, the CPA embarked upon this collaborative endeavour with Wilton Park to hold joint annual conferences, which has proved to be such a beneficial combination and has produced such worthwhile and useful results.

I am haunted by a sense that I have fallen short of properly reflecting the treasure-trove of ideas that were debated during that memorable week in June 2001. Such failings are entirely mine. For what there is of value in the ensuing chapters, I must thank the presenters, whose work has furnished the backbone of what follows, and the conference participants, whose comments and questions during both the workshops and plenary discussions did so much to illuminate the issues at hand.

I must express my sincere gratitude to Mr Donahoe for having enough confidence in my abilities to allow me to undertake this work in the first place. May I also thank Mr Nicholas Hopkinson, Deputy Director of Wilton Park, not only for his kindness and assistance throughout, but for providing me with copies of much of the material he has written over the years, which proved to be so enormously useful to me in this endeavour. I also thank Mr Anthony Staddon of the CPA Secretariat for his never-ending patience and continuous assistance. Finally, may I add my very special thanks to my husband Gregory Traversy for reading drafts and final texts and offering such useful comments and helpful editorial assistance, and for putting up with me throughout the entire process.

# 1 Introduction: democracy, parliaments and electoral systems

> Parliamentary democracy may not be perfect but something would be badly wrong if the people and media were not openly and healthily sceptical about the democratic system and were not debating on how to improve it.

With these thoughts, Nicholas Hopkinson ended his book *Parliamentary Democracy: Is There a Perfect Model?*, which is based upon the joint Commonwealth Parliamentary Association/Wilton Park Conference on that theme which took place in February 1999. As the ensuing chapters will attest, there was an abundance of debate on how to improve democracy and its supporting parliamentary and electoral infrastructure at the subsequent CPA/Wilton Park Conference on 'Democracy, Parliament and Electoral Systems' which is the focus of this volume.

Moreover, in many parts of the world, there persists no shortage of scepticism about the merits of democratic governance. On these grounds, at least, I hope we are entitled to take some comfort in the thought that all is not 'badly wrong'.

Such comfort is in decidedly scarcer supply as these lines are being penned in early November 2001, than was the case when the conference took place. Seen against the tragic backdrop of September 11, and the ensuing military conflict, the world we share appears, at least for the time being, a darker and less promising one than the one that beckoned from outside the windows of Wilton House in June 2001.

By contrast, the relevance of the conference's themes is more sharply illuminated against this sombre background than before. As Sir Winston Churchill stated in a speech given in 1947, 'Many forms of government have been tried, and will be tried in this world of sin and woe. No one pretends that democracy is perfect or all-wise. Indeed, it has been said that democracy is the worst form of government except all those other forms that have been tried from time to time.' To defend democratic government is to accept that it is by no means perfect. It is to realise at the same time, however, that to run a successful state or nation, power must be exercised by some over others, by the few over the many, and that democracy can allow the views of those concerned on any significant issue to be aired and taken into account before decisions are taken. It will allow the many to feel they are not powerless to affect the actions of government. In the worst case, the people can at least express their views against perceived bad decisions taken by a government at the next election, by voting them out of office and giving power to someone else.

The procedures for allowing public input may be costly, cumbersome and time-consuming, whether it is the holding of elections or the canvassing of views on issues or maintaining the infrastructure required to run the system. No one would suggest otherwise. The alternative however, is simply worse.

The specific shapes and forms of democracy are as diverse as the free nations of the world. Parliaments around the globe vary greatly. They are unicameral and bicameral, unitary states and federal ones, single party, two party, multi-party, and a few with no political parties at all. There are legislatures with less than twenty members and others with over a thousand. The electoral systems, by which the members of legislatures are chosen, also differ enormously from majority systems to proportional, modified proportional and mixed systems. Yet, even with so many differences, it is the commonalties that are the more significant features, the glue that binds together all those who, like the conference participants, are committed to the continuing quest for improving our shared 'worst system of government'.

The sections of the volume that follows correspond to the main themes of the conference. Correspondingly, Part I explores the avenues and approaches for building democracy, both at the level of such fundamental principles as transparency and integrity, and at the level of possible, specific, practical initiatives. It also includes a country-based case study of a transition from totalitarianism to democracy. Part II examines the scope for improving the effectiveness of parliaments and legislatures. It explores once again both broader structural and procedural approaches and the more specific technical and operational opportunities offered by information technology.

Parts III and IV focus on electoral systems. Part III examines broader cross-cutting issues and alternatives. It looks at the mechanics of holding elections and at various potential influences on election results, both internal and external. Part IV provides a wealth of country-based insights and experiences with various electoral systems that are both positive and negative.

In the struggle to reflect properly the many insights provided by the conference's presenters, my thoughts have often turned to the long traditions of effort by both the Commonwealth Parliamentary Association and Wilton Park to forge and sustain a global community of commitment to better governance. It is more important than ever that those efforts continue. The chapters that follow are intended to contribute to that ongoing quest.

# PART I

## BUILDING DEMOCRACY

# 2 Enhancing democracy: a Caribbean perspective

*This chapter is based on a paper presented by Professor Selwyn Ryan, University of the West Indies, St Augustine, Trinidad, and on the ensuing discussions in workshop and plenary sessions.*

There has been a large amount of research and writing by academics on the utility of transplanting the competitive, adversarial, Western form of democracy to newly independent states. Transitions from military dictatorships or other forms of authoritarian government to functioning democracies, with 'free and fair' elections, independent judiciaries, freedom of the press, and bureaucracies where transparency and accountability are the fundamental underpinnings, are clearly not effortless changes even under the best of circumstances.

## Theories of change

Various theories of social change seek to explain the ability successfully to alter an existing governance system in the direction of democracy. Some argue that class structure or ethnic identities inhibit change. Some assert that all choices are predominately influenced by what has gone before and that institutional forces shape political goals and directions of change. Others emphasise the role of chance as a major factor, with developments such as the emergence of a charismatic leader, a social crisis or an external event playing the key role. Still others stress the combination of interactive factors which are at play in any specific situation, noting that barriers which in some cases prove impossible to overcome, in other somewhat similar cases are significantly modified through concerted action to permit evolution in the desired direction. All would agree, however, that to effect and sustain change of the scope and scale required to make the transition to democracy successfully requires both material and human resources in significant measure and in combination with other ingredients. How have these theories translated into practice in various parts of the world?

### Caribbean experience

The Caribbean has long been thought to have made the transition to democracy successfully. Since 1962 when Jamaica and Trinidad and Tobago achieved independence, ten of the twelve anglophone Caribbean countries have consistently been free of unconstitutional transfers of power. A majority of these countries have also had at least one election where the opposition party successfully defeated the governing party, and power was peacefully turned over. Does this mean that the Westminster style of democracy has successfully been transplanted to the Caribbean? Many Caribbean scholars would argue it has not.

Because of the small size of the various islands, it is argued that it is very difficult to prevent political abuse in the Caribbean. Everyone is dependent upon the government for something. Everyone knows everyone else and for that reason they are usually reluctant to give offence. Corruption, when it does occur, is difficult to counter. Police and civil servants may fear for their jobs or not wish to hurt family or friends.

I was reminded during Professor Ryan's presentation of a visit I took many years ago to a small Caribbean island. A conversation with a local businessman made the problems of size vividly real when he began talking about his nephew. This boy of twenty had recently returned home from another nearby island, and on passing through customs he was found to be carrying illegal drugs. The customs officer in charge that day was another uncle, who after turning his nephew over to police had to phone his sister, the boy's mother, to tell her about the arrest. When everyone knows everyone else and is either family or a friend, just doing your job can be enormously difficult.

It is easy to forget that a system that works well in a large country may not transplant easily to a very small one without adjustments. In a small face-to-face society most people are reluctant to 'make waves', to hurt family or friends, or to jeopardise the status quo. This translates from day-to-day living into the society as a whole.

### Winner takes all?

In the political sphere is the 'winner takes all' approach well-suited to a small close-knit society? Would a more inclusive, less adversarial way of governing work better? Should, for example, consideration be given to changing the electoral system, at least in one house where the parliament is bicameral, to some form of proportional representation, in order to allow for more parties to be elected, obtain broader representation and accommodate the need for more consensus and cooperation? Where corruption exists, it would be harder to maintain it when many more players need to be consulted and involved in order to govern.

The goal in government should always be to improve the quality of life for the population as a whole. Ways need to be found to build safeguards into the system to ensure that goal is met.

### Westminster pros and cons

Some feel that the Westminster model does not work well because many of the unwritten underpinnings of the British model are not easy to transfer to another culture. Others feel it is working reasonably well, and as well as could be expected in such small countries. They feel that what is needed are merely small, incremental changes to improve the day-to-day functioning of the system, not a major change in system.

[ 9 ]

The Westminster model is one that is now familiar in the English-speaking Caribbean. Both the benefits and the problems are evident. There are those who advocate moving to a congressional system with its formal built-in separation of powers, feeling that this would ensure greater cooperation between the executive and the legislature. In their view it would strengthen the elected houses, thereby softening the 'one person rule' problem that now exists in many countries. A charismatic and long-serving prime minister is often less and less likely to be consultative and compromise-oriented as time goes on. There are those who feel this can only be changed with a change in system.

Others, in fact the majority, are of the view that by adjusting the existing Westminster model, Caribbean countries could be governed more effectively within existing structures. They feel that the key to achieving better government is cultural and political change, not constitutional change. In their view, the old 'plantation mentality' where authoritarianism was endemic is still too prevalent in many areas, and needs to change in order to permit evolution to a more democratic type of governance.

Is the mood now ripe for creating, implementing and sustaining meaningful change in the Caribbean? If the consensus exists on the need for change, are the required resources available, both enough money and the right people? If the answer to both these questions is yes, what needs to be done?

### Suggestions for improvement

Many suggestions have been made as to how the existing Westminster model could be adapted to fit the smaller-sized English-speaking Caribbean countries, to strengthen their systems and make them more accountable. Some of the following ideas have been tried in some countries with varying degrees of success, while others are still in the discussion stage. These suggestions come from a number of experts throughout the Caribbean and elsewhere.

1. Limiting the number of terms that a leader can remain in power, as for example is the case with the American President (only two terms allowed), is one proposal. It is felt that by requiring more frequent changes in leadership, a more equitable power sharing among the political elite would ensue.

2. As many countries now have an ombudsman, strengthening this role by providing more resources, both material and financial, and more independence from the executive, is suggested as a way to strengthen democracy. Given financial independence, this agency would be able to monitor the administration and intervene when required to minimise abuse.

3. Establishing or, where they already exist, strengthening parliamentary committees that have an oversight role is another suggested way to improve the accountability of government. For example:

   • A Public Accounts Committee, with a mandated role to review and report on government spending, particularly when chaired by an experienced opposition member, can assist in providing a check on government operations.

   • A Regulations and Statutory Instruments Committee which overviews and comments on the implementation of government legislation, with the power to trigger debates on regulations it finds problematic by recommending revocation, is another suggested measure to strengthen accountability.

   • Requirements for oversight built into the system and given adequate resources independent from the executive can serve as a useful monitoring mechanism, which can focus public attention on problems in their early stages and help curtail abuse.

   • Establishing or empowering parliamentary committees to monitor and review the spending and operations of government departments and state owned corporations is another useful tool. Responsible ministers, appointed heads and bureaucrats can be called to appear regularly as witnesses before these committees. The requirement for reports to be tabled on their operations and effectiveness is another suggestion for improved accountability.

4. Restricting the number of parliamentarians who may be appointed to the executive to 50 per cent or less of the total parliamentary membership would strengthen the role of oversight committees by increasing the number of backbenchers available to serve. Sufficient numbers of both government and opposition members must be available to work on these committees. Where membership in the lower house is extremely small, it could be increased to at least twenty-four to allow for sufficient members to fill both executive and backbench rolls. This would also provide for better constituency representation. The provision whereby governments have an automatic majority in the Senate could also be abolished where it now exists.

5. An independent electoral officer, adequately funded and staffed separately from government, whose role is to run elections independently from political parties and government, is a suggested reform. The power to invite local and international observers, prior to, during and immediately following elections is also suggested as an important mechanism to ensure fairness. The presence of and subsequent report from monitoring groups would assist those trying to provide for free and fair elections and could serve to discourage electoral malpractice.

6. It has also been suggested that the media should be privately owned and operated. Moreover, it is further suggested that, where the media is state owned, it should be privatised and made to compete, or should operate totally at arms length from the government, with strictly enforced rules for balanced coverage of all political views and fair limits on election coverage for all candidates.

7. A professional public service, which is able to balance loyalty requirements to the government in power with the autonomy required to function fairly and in an apolitical manner, is a suggested requirement. To assist in maintaining public service neutrality, the use of special advisers to Ministers, who would have an explicitly politically partisan role, could be encouraged.

8. Ensuring that government contracts are awarded fairly and through a competitive process, by establishing an agency or Contractor General to monitor and report to Parliament regularly, is another suggestion.

9. The introduction of aspects of proportional representation, particularly in the upper house, to compensate for the under representation of smaller parties and minority groups in the lower house, is another reform proposal. A mixture of first-past-the-post and proportional representation, as in the German model, could strengthen accountability.

10. Giving the head of state a greater role in the appointment of officials to sensitive national offices and regulatory institutions and/or giving parliamentary committees the power to call nominees as witnesses before their appointment (perhaps with the power to veto appointments with just cause) are further possible initiatives.

11. Consideration could be given to amendments to legislation or standing orders of legislatures requiring parliamentarians elected for one political party to resign their seats should they change to other parties during a parliament.

12. Senior public servants, heads of state enterprises and members of statutory bodies and commissions could be allowed to complete their term of office regardless of a change of government. Automatic resignation, which exists now in some countries with Westminster-type democracies despite the fact that it is not part of the Westminster model, would be abolished.

Some may argue that the cost of many of the suggested reforms is a problem. However, it must be kept in mind that not all are required at once. In addition, the expense required would be far less than the cost of significant political unrest or of major constitutional change, which may be the result if nothing is done.

## Westminster implementation problems

Small societies experience two significant problems implementing the Westminster model of parliament. First, the limited number of human resources in parliament makes it hard to have sufficient numbers of experienced politicians to staff adequately both the government and opposition ranks, in order to provide strong government and effective opposition. Particularly if oversight committees are to form a substantial part of the accountability structure, sufficient numbers of backbench members from both sides of the house are essential.

Second, there needs to be a loosening of party discipline to allow and even encourage occasional dissent by members in all parties on various issues, without the risk of reprisals or accusations of disloyalty. Tolerance of criticism, while difficult to engender in small parliaments, is needed to allow for a wider range of views to be aired on issues. Experience suggests that good government requires consistent testing from both outside and within its structure, to ensure that the best paths are being followed.

### Suggestions for change

Increasing slightly the number of seats in some legislatures might help, by increasing the number of members available to serve as the 'conscience' of those in positions of power. Such an increase must be combined with rules to limit the numbers of members in the executive, and an effort at changing the attitude towards constructive criticism and alternative proposals. The personalised competition between politicians that often now exists needs to give way to more impersonal national discussion of ideas and issues without fear of accusations of disloyalty but rather praise for courage and independence.

In some parts of the Caribbean there have been strong suggestions for more radical constitutional and electoral changes. In Jamaica, from the 1980s to the mid-1990s, there was discussion of retention or replacement of the monarchy as head of state. Many argued it was time to break the psychological link between the Jamaican people and the British Crown. While there were many who agreed that the time was ripe for such a move, there was little agreement on what the new structure of government should look like.

Some preferred to retain the Westminster system, strengthening it through the addition of oversight committees with other structural modifications in order to monitor and scrutinise the executive. By allowing for greater authority for parliament over the executive, it was felt by some that the existing system could be improved. The appointment of a non-executive president, who represented no political party, as head of state was also suggested as part of this proposal.

Others favoured a more drastic revision along the lines of the American model, with the executive presidential role being incorporated in one person. Some feared this would concentrate too much power in the hands of the executive, and worried this new position would be even more powerful than the existing prime minister.

Still others suggested retention of the prime minister role but with direct election by the people and the incumbent limited to two five-year terms. Elections to the legislature and senate would be held separately from that for prime minister. Other positions such as speaker of the house and president of the senate would be elected by their respective houses. Both houses would elect officers such as the commissioner of police and members of the Service Commission. These proposals were criticised by some as potentially leading to deadlock, while others felt they would foster greater cooperation and help to build consensus.

Additional reforms suggested that all members should be available to work in constituency offices that would be totally separate from political offices and be entirely funded by the state. In those offices, the members would serve all their constituents regardless of political party allegiance.

### Power sharing

In an ethnically heterogeneous society, the question of power sharing is one that arises consistently. Problems of alienation and demands for justice from all groups are common. The 'winner take all' aspect of the Westminster system needs to be modified to include more consensual possibilities in such cases.

Those in power, or with strong hopes of forming a government, are usually loath to change the existing system in any fundamental way. It tends to be those with little hope of gaining power who are the strongest advocates of change. However, when the population at large feels totally disenfranchised and comes to the view that elections are meaningless exercises where they have no viable choice in how they are governed, alternative structures or systems or modifications to the status quo must ultimately ensue.

## Looking ahead

One of the aspects of change that is currently being experienced, not only in the Caribbean but other parts of the world as well, is the death of the 'old order'. Political affiliations based on class, religion, race and colour are lessening. In England, France and Germany, parties once based on class are disappearing, declining or rebranding. English society is becoming more complex. Class voting has fallen significantly, with the electorate now supporting parties based more on leadership and the parties' stand on various policy issues.

This decoupling of class and party is also to be seen in Jamaica and the eastern Caribbean, where labour parties are now being led by university-trained intelligentsia and are attracting trans-class support. More and more frequently the new generation of voters are choosing to move their vote depending upon issues and leaders, and a new volatility in the electorate is evident. In Trinidad and Tobago and in Guyana, this phenomenon is apparently less evident.

With respect to political models in the Caribbean, there is a widespread innate conservatism and suspicion of change. The disenchantment lies less with the system of government than with the players. The Westminster system is known and respected, and retains legitimacy with most of the populace.

It would therefore follow that incremental reforms would be the most easily acceptable and have the best hope for success. It must be kept in mind that no change can be contemplated without considering all the interrelated factors, and that what works for one does not necessarily work for all. Finally, the effect of the change on other related aspects of governance must be thought through carefully before implementation, in order that uncontemplated surprises do not defeat the original intent.

# 3 Transparency, integrity and funding of the political process

*This section is based upon a paper presented by Mr Jeremy Pope, Executive Director, Transparency International, London, and on the subsequent plenary discussion.*

For an elected legislature to function as watchdog, regulator and representative, it must be at the centre of the struggle to attain and sustain good governance and fight corruption. To have the respect and confidence of the electorate, it must be composed of individuals of integrity.

### Accountability mechanisms

Democracies are better able than other political systems to deter corruption through institutionalised checks and balances,and other meaningful accountability mechanisms. Such processes can open up the activities of public officials to public scrutiny and accountability. Through transparency and openness, corruption can be reduced in its extent, significance and pervasiveness.

The holding of free and fair elections allows the public to choose individuals of integrity to represent them and to vote against those who abuse their position. Elections are, of course, but one step in the process of democratic government. Effective, ongoing oversight is essential throughout a parliament.

### Political parties

In virtually all parliamentary democracies, political parties play a key role. They can be seen to serve a number of functions. They can contribute to internal stability by allowing various groups to participate in the political process in an orderly and predictable manner. They provide an orderly means for the legitimate transfer of power from one group to another. They can play a major role in the selection, training, grooming and promotion of politicians.

A few states operate without the formal existence of political parties. For example, at the present time Uganda, the Channel Islands, the Northwest Territories and Nunavut in Canada do not recognise political parties. In most countries, however, political parties seem to evolve naturally. Groups of individuals tend to congregate around a specific leader with whom they share particular lines of political thought.

Political parties are private organisations that control their own membership and seek political rather than financial profit. Parties are however expensive to operate. They need money for offices and staff, for deposits for candidates, and to communicate with the public. They need money to run election campaigns and to monitor all aspects of the election process itself, to ensure that it is being run fairly.

### Funding requirements

To finance their activities, they need to raise money. While their supporters can be called upon to contribute, small donations from large numbers of individuals are expensive to collect. In most democracies, the principal source of funding for political parties is the private sector. Companies and individuals contribute for a variety of reasons, but almost certainly in the hope of obtaining access to and attention from the leadership. They may also expect patronage if the party succeeds in winning office, perhaps by way of appointment to a public office or consideration in the awarding of contracts. Companies may contribute to both sides of the political spectrum because they realise money is required for the process, and they are in effect supporting the public good by supporting the process. At the same time, they are staying in favour with whichever party gets elected.

If political parties are to play a key role in virtually every legislative system, their method of funding will be extremely significant. It is important that the fundraising processes do not distort the political system to favour only those with access to money. Mechanisms need to be put in place to monitor and report on the situation. Knowing who has contributed significant amounts to specific political parties is an important safeguard in preventing corruption.

In many countries, it is felt that in order to relieve political parties from their total dependence on the private sector for their existence, it is necessary to institute state funding. However, even countries with generous state funding of political parties, have not been free of scandals. In Germany, for example, the outgoing head of government has consistently refused to disclose the identities of those who funded him over the years, on the grounds of promised confidentiality.

In instances where the funding process is not transparent and political parties are free to not disclose the sources of sizeable donations, then the public will draw its own conclusions, basing their speculation on where they see lucrative government contracts being awarded. Mechanisms and guidelines must be in place to regulate donations, and severe penalties for infractions must be directly tied to specific infractions.

A formula that can be seen to be equitable is required for public funding of political parties. Every party cannot be funded equally, for it would hardly be fair to fund a small party to the same extent as a major national party. One method used in some countries is to allocate public funds in proportion to the votes won at the last election.

## Limiting expenses

Best practices would suggest that expenses should be limited but reasonable. If limits are too low, they will be ignored. Set too high, they encourage excess. Some general guidelines that could be followed are as follows:

- Campaign length should be kept reasonably short: not so short as to favour the party currently in power, but not so long as to produce very high campaign costs.
- Grants from public funds should be made according to an agreed formula, and administered by an independent Electoral Commission (for example, in accordance with past election performance).
- There should be strict limits on contributions of both cash and services. Such limits need to be reasonable and should be disclosed.
- Both parties and candidates should have limits imposed on what they may spend during an election campaign. They should be required to submit an audited account of their expenditures in both cash and kind within sixty days following the election to the Election Commission. Those failure to submit, or found guilty of making false declarations or over-expenditure, should face stiff penalties decided upon and publicised well in advance of the election.
- In Canada, for example, Parliament has passed laws relating to bribery and corruption in elections, delegating to the courts the power to determine whether breaches have occurred. Where a candidate is found guilty of some form of corruption, penalties may include several years of disqualification from candidacy in subsequent elections; fines, imprisonment, or both; or the loss of the right to sit or vote in the House.
- Political parties should be required to file annual audited accounts of income at electorate, regional and national levels.
- Anonymous donations should be prohibited, and should be either returned or sent directly to the Electoral Commission.
- Controls should be in place before elections, for fair and acceptable levels of paid-for radio and television advertising. The Electoral

Commission should determine the limits for free time radio and television broadcasts for each political party during a campaign.

## Legislated safeguards

Safeguards against corruption in funding for political parties should not relate merely to the election campaign period. Once in office, members of the legislature must be held accountable for their exercise of power. The legislators who make the laws should not themselves be above the law.

Australia, for example, added a section to the Federal Crimes Act in 1982, that makes it an offence punishable by imprisonment for two years, for a member of either House of Parliament, to ask for or receive any property or benefit on the understanding that the exercise of his or her duty or authority as a member would in any way be influenced or affected. A person who promises or offers such a benefit is also subject to the same law and the same punishment.

## Crossing the floor

In many legislatures, members elected as representatives of one political party are free to 'cross the floor' and join another, whether their constituents agree or not. The thinking behind this is that their electors may pronounce upon the decision at the next election. What occurred in some cases however, was legislators being persuaded to leave their original party by offers of large sums of money, promises of appointments, or other such incentives.

In India defections became so widespread that in 1985, the government found it necessary to pass the 52nd Amendment to the Constitution which was, in effect, an anti-defection law. It provided that an elected member would be disqualified from being a member if he or she joined another political party. There was, however, the provision that while individual acts of defection were prevented, defections en masse were still allowed. A group of members is allowed to split away from one party provided the

[ 23 ]

group consists of not less than one-third of the members of such a legislature party. Disqualification on the grounds of defection also does not apply in the case of mergers, where a member's original party merges with another party and not less than two-thirds of the members of the party concerned agree to such a merger.

By-elections are also now required in Malawi and in Trinidad and Tobago when a sitting member changes parties.

Normally, in proportional representation systems, when a member changes parties, he or she is automatically replaced by the next name on the list. This provision was not included in the new proportional system recently introduced in New Zealand, a situation that has caused some recent difficulties there. (Note: This is discussed more fully in Chapter 17 on the New Zealand experience of changing electoral systems.)

### A bottom line

The public is sceptical about politics and politicians at the best of times. If it is ensured that there are built-in accountability mechanisms, regular full disclosure practices, ongoing monitoring and independent oversight bodies, the public will be reassured that their democratic institutions are being justly and fairly run.

# 4 The Spanish transition: dictatorship to democracy

*This section is based on a presentation by Senator Esperanza Aguirre Gil de Biedma, Speaker of the Senate, Madrid, Spain, and on the associated discussions.*

The period 1976 to 1978 marked the transition from dictatorship to democracy for Spain. In June 1977 Spain held its first democratic election since the civil war. Nine members were elected from existing political parties to become a committee whose mandate was to draft a new Constitution for Spain. All nine are still alive today and many of them are still involved in Parliament.

### Constitutional Committee

The Constitutional Committee presented its report in 1978, making detailed recommendations on the structure of a new system of government for Spain. A lively debate on the report then ensued. It was decided to put the question of acceptance of the report's recommendations to the people by means of a national referendum. Because the public was consulted by this means, the issue of how the government would be structured was widely and openly debated. The process ensured an opportunity for the public to become aware of the possibilities and involved in the decision. They therefore largely bought into the new system right from the beginning.

The acceptance level for the constitutional proposals in the committee report was an overwhelming 88 per cent in favour.

Accordingly, in July 1978, the Spanish Constitutional Accord was agreed to.

### Spanish Parliament

There are two houses in the Parliament, and both the Congress and the Senate are elected on a proportional basis. The Senate is the chamber of regional representation, and is elected every four years on a mixed system, with some senators directly elected and other indirectly. Those who are directly elected are chosen on a simple majority vote from lists compiled at the provincial level. The senators indirectly elected are chosen by the legislative assemblies of the autonomous communities, according to their own rules of procedure, on a proportional basis.

For the directly elected senators there are fifty-two multi-member constituencies, which correspond to the country's provinces, and the two African city territories of Ceuta and Melilla. The provinces elect three or four senators each, depending upon size. For the island provinces, each island or grouping with a representation or insular council comprises a voting district for the purpose of electing senators. The major islands – Grand Canary, Mallorca and Tenerife – elect three senators each. The smaller islands or island groupings – Ibiza-Formentera, Menorca, Fuerteventura, Gomera, Hierro, Lanzarote and La Palma – elect one senator each. The city territories of Ceuta and Melilla elect two senators each.

For the indirectly elected senators, each of the seventeen autonomous communities returns one senator, plus one additional senator for each 1 000 000 inhabitants. The legislative assembly of each community, or in its absence the higher collective body of the community pursuant to statute, chooses these senators.

In total there are 259 senators at the present time, with 200 elected by the provinces and the remaining fifty-nine chosen by the regional parliaments.

The senate provides a legitimate and democratic forum to represent the various regional and territorial interests of the country. This has helped to solidify national unity in Spain and has gone a long way to resolving problems of regional, linguistic and cultural differences, which have plagued Spain in the past.

## The Basque issue

The Basque issue continues to be problematic. Regrettably, total independence and separation from Spain is the only solution that the Basque separatists seem willing to consider, a solution Spain as a whole is unwilling to contemplate. As a result, it is difficult to envisage a solution that will prove satisfactory to all.

Some people argue that a federalist system might help to improve the Basque situation, on the grounds that if all regions were to be equal, this would go further along to road to providing the Basques with the autonomy they are seeking. The system of self-governing regions that now exists is neither federal nor centralised. In addition, the two federal Houses are asymmetrical. They are chosen by different systems, and in the case of a dispute between the two, Congress will prevail. Both Houses do, however, share both a legislative role and an oversight of government function.

## Bicameralism

There has also been criticism by some of the bicameralism of the Spanish Parliament. Some maintain that unicameralism is a more efficient form of government, more cost-effective and more efficient. They question whether it is really necessary to have a bicameral national parliament when the provinces and regions of the country all have their own governments.

The answer to this question is that having a forum for dialogue where, in an atmosphere of mutual respect, consensus can be sought on regional and provincial matters, is probably too valuable an entity to sacrifice to the mere goals of saving either time or money.

## A successful transition

Spain has come a long way down the road of democracy in the twenty-three years since the adoption of the Constitutional Accord. Economic development since its implementation has been unprecedented. It would probably be extremely unwise to tamper too significantly with a system that has produced such obviously positive results.

# PART II

---

# MAKING PARLIAMENTS MORE EFFECTIVE

# 5 Strengthening parliament's role

*This section is based upon a paper presented by Lord Norton of Louth, Professor of Government, University of Hull, United Kingdom and on the associated discussions that followed.*

### Parliaments and legislatures

The most usual definition of a parliament encompasses the sovereign or head of state, and the legislative arm, either unicameral or bicameral, working in tandem. The government, the opposition and the backbenchers from both sides make up the players in the house or houses of parliament, with the government being composed of a prime minister and cabinet ministers who have seats in the legislature, most commonly in the elected lower house.

The legislative arm in the Westminster model differs fundamentally from those in a congressional system, in that the executive, including the prime minister, are members of the legislative arm in the Westminster model and must maintain the confidence of that body in order to govern. In the congressional model the president and cabinet are completely separate from the legislative arm. The executive and legislative arms must work together in order for laws to be passed and policy to be implemented.

They are different systems working in different ways but with many basic similarities. In fact, the general population will frequently see the similarities and forget the differences. They may suggest incorporating components of one system into the other, seeing them as desirable features that are lacking in their own system, or they may advocate changing their system completely in favour of the other 'better' system. These are complex questions requiring careful thought and consideration, but there is little doubt that learning from the experiences of others is a useful practice, which saves both time and effort.

What then is a legislature, a common feature to both the Westminster and congressional systems? In broad general terms what does it do? How do its powers vary throughout the world? How are they similar? Where legislatures play a relatively weak role in the governing process, how can that role be strengthened in order to make the governments more accountable?

A legislature can generally be defined as a body of persons invested with the powers to make or enact the laws of a country or state. Legislatures are basically deliberative assemblies, where the issues of the day are discussed and laws are made and amended. They all tend to be multifunctional entities, with a wide variety of roles such as assenting to taxes being imposed, considering and approving how the government spends money, debating and voting on policy issues, passing new laws and amending existing ones. Their powers will vary not only in what they do, but also in the extent to which they can initiate matters or change proposals that are put before them. Although their functions can be modified and altered over time, the core function central to all is assenting to legislation.

Variations in the powers of legislatures are not a subject that lends itself easily to invariant explanations because so many factors can be at play. Within a single legislature, with no change whatsoever in rules or procedures, the legislature's functioning might vary widely from one election to another. Does the party in power have a large majority or a narrow one? Are parties governing within a coalition? Does the prime minister of the day have a consultative approach or a more authoritarian method? Is he or she a strong parliamentarian with a great appreciation for the legislature's role, or does he or she view it rather as an obstacle that must be dealt with? Is the economy strong or is the financial situation in the country problematic? So many different factors can influence how a legislature will operate that any theory to explain it must be applied cautiously. General theories are, however, useful in helping focus our thinking on the functions and operations of legislative bodies from the perspective of comparing one with another and comparing the same legislature to itself over time.

### Policy-making role of legislatures

Starting from this perspective, all legislatures in the world could be grouped into three broad categories. First are those that make policy, such as the United States Congress, as well as the various state legislatures in the USA. They have not only the power to consider, amend and concur in or reject measures brought forth by the executive, but also the power to initiate and formulate their own policies. The number of legislatures in the world that either have or use this power to initiate legislation to any great extent is not large. However, it is increasing, as for example in Central and Eastern Europe.

At the opposite end of the spectrum are those legislatures with virtually no powers to amend or affect policy. Legislatures in Communist regimes or those found in single-party states would make up the preponderance of legislative bodies in this category. It is a small group of countries, which has grown smaller in recent years with the collapse of communism in the USSR, and the expansion of multi-party democracies in Africa.

The third, and by far the largest, group comprises those legislatures that influence policy through amending or rejecting legislation, but lack the capacity either to formulate or substitute their own policies or to bring their own ideas into effect to any significant degree. Virtually all Commonwealth countries and most Western European countries fall into this large group.

Many factors influence which type of legislature a country has, the prime ones being the political culture of the nation, its constitution and its electoral and party system. While legislatures themselves can change the degree to which they influence policy, the move from policy influencing to policy making would come about only as a result of changes external to the legislature itself.

This middle ground of policy influencing is occupied by most of the legislatures in the world. They can change or amend or reject legislation, but do not play any significant role in initiating it. The role they do play varies enormously from country to country. It is also one that can vary within a legislature over a period of time, either strengthening or weakening, and it is one that legislators themselves have the power to influence and to alter.

### Effectiveness of legislatures

There is the perception among many legislators themselves that their powers have decreased over the years. In the British Parliament for example, the Report of the Commission to Strengthen Parliament, published in July 2000, cited various developments that have served to weaken the role played by the House of Commons. Such things as the growth of party loyalty and cohesion, the enormous increase in both the quantity and quality of legislation dealt with by the House and the growth of organised interests, have all contributed to both the lack of time necessary and the ability of Members to influence legislation. They simply do not have the time to deal adequately with every issue before them with any level of depth. The ability to provide a significant influence requires the time to talk to people, to prepare arguments, to acquire details and facts in order to persuade and caution. With too much to do, proper consideration cannot be given to all items considered.

Other factors that have been identified as contributing to the diminishing effectiveness of the British house are the increase in partisanship; the increasing concentration of power in the prime minister, making him or her more detached from his/her own party and Parliament; and constitutional change which has removed some law-making powers to other institutions, such as the European Parliament and other elected assemblies in the UK.

Other countries should be aware that factors such as those listed above increase the risk of diminishing the effectiveness of legislatures in holding governments accountable. Adapting to change in such circumstances is essential to safeguarding the effectiveness of a parliament.

### The scope for constructive change

How can change best be initiated, and what types of change are possible?

Sometimes change will be driven by the population as a whole. With widespread public dissatisfaction, fuelled by a persistent media, and academic support, the existing democratic government will find it necessary to initiate change, even if it personally does not favour it. Commissions will then be appointed, or committees struck, to look into the issue and provide recommendations. Public consultations and fact-finding exercises will help to define possibilities. Referenda or other consultative methods will further refine choices. When action is finally taken on changes of this nature, there is normally strong support, and the new initiative has a strong chance of success as a result. Change of this type is infrequent, but will normally be significant in scope and impact.

The more usual change exercises are initiated internally to a legislature and result from imbalances that are proving troublesome to the day-to-day functioning. They often arise after an election has changed the make-up of the house, and the status quo has been altered to the extent that continuing as before proves difficult. A change in government often presents such an occasion, when new leadership arrives with new ideas about how things should be done.

Even without a new party in power, an election can alter the size of a government majority, perhaps producing a larger number of backbenchers eager for a meaningful role. With more resources available, using a sizeable backbench in a meaningful way becomes a new priority both for the members themselves and for the government. A review exercise leading to a change in powers or functions will frequently result.

Any type of change to a legislature needs the support of the players involved in order to be effective. The degree of change that can be brought about by the members themselves can be a substantial increase of powers within their existing category of legislature. Moving from one category to another, or changing types of electoral system, or any other such overriding changes, will always be driven initially from outside the legislature. Having said that, what can the members of a legislature do themselves to enhance their powers and increase their effectiveness?

Changes can both positively and negatively affect the powers of legislatures. In fact, a decrease in specific powers can also be a force for improvement. Removing specific responsibilities from a legislature and having them dealt with elsewhere, by a provincial or territorial government for example, can free a legislature to concentrate more on other issues. Giving up powers is not necessarily a bad thing, if it means providing the time and means to strengthen the legislature's role in other more significant areas.

*Specialisation*

In a large legislature, the sheer size can be an inhibitor to effectiveness. This can be countered through the specialisation of members and the use of committees. As legislation becomes more complex and voluminous, a degree of specialisation among the elected members goes a long way to enhancing the effectiveness of scrutiny. Members can choose areas of interest, and concentrate on becoming experts in two or three specific fields. They will enhance their knowledge in a given subject area by serving on a particular committee for an extended period of time, by having access to expert advice independent of the executive, and by having the time needed to devote to understanding the issues in depth. They can then influence business to a far greater extent.

Parliaments that have a consistently high turnover in membership are at a serious disadvantage in having a sufficient number of experienced members with enough expertise to provide meaningful input into the scrutiny role. The ideal mix of experience and fresh ideas is best available in a legislature of reasonable size with a moderate turnover of membership. Unfortunately, this is an ideal situation that is difficult to guarantee.

A legislature that is extremely small will simply not have enough variety in backgrounds and expertise in its membership, nor enough warm bodies to fulfil all the necessary functions well. People will be stretched too thin to do everything that is necessary. In some legislatures, increasing membership sufficiently to provide for a better balance of expertise might be a necessary requirement if it is to become more effective.

At the other extreme, a very large legislature can also prove to be ineffective. A large body, meeting in plenary, is simply not an effective group for detailed scrutiny. The creation of small committees, with extensive powers of agenda setting, amendment and evidence taking, adequately supported by administrative and research services, will strengthen the role of these legislatures. A small group can either be formed from members with existing expertise in an area, or the group can develop and enhance its expertise through continuity of membership on a particular committee for an extended period.

*Committee reform*

Allowing subject matter committees to initiate studies provides a level of independence from the executive, and can serve as a safety valve on contentious issues of the day. Committees given the power to travel within a state or country can bring the democratic process closer to the people and allow for direct public input. The members are then acting as a direct link between the electorate and the executive. They will hear first-hand the views of the public on a specific issue, and can pass their information back immediately to the executive in parliament. A committee meeting within a region of the country can also enhance the very necessary educative role that members must play in relation to the parliamentary process, and to the very idea of change being brought about through debate and compromise within the democratic process.

Providing for permanent parliamentary committees with stable memberships and access to independent resources can serve to strengthen the oversight role of the legislature. Effective committees of a legislature will be more effective bodies and more able to keep governments accountable if they incorporate a number of features. These are:

### SMALL SIZE

A small committee will be more apt to become less politically partisan, and better able to find common ground that can be achieved through working together. More will get done faster, with fewer people to speak on every issue. Members come to know each other better, and as a result they will be more able to give and take on an issue and find compromise solutions to problems.

### PERMANENCE

Setting up the committees at the beginning of a parliament, and keeping them functioning for an entire session, or possibly for the life of a parliament, is important in building the expertise of the membership. In addition, a stable membership is equally important in order for the members to become knowledgeable in the field and to have influence. With minimum explanations required, the committees can then question proposals in detail and suggest and defend significant improvements.

### AN INFORMED MEMBERSHIP

When members are chosen for committees, previous experience or study in the particular field of specialisation is an enormous benefit to enhance the expertise of the group as a whole. It will also help to provide greater credibility to the reports and recommendations that the committee produces.

### DEPARTMENTAL PARALLELS

It is important that the committee structure provide for committees that mirror as exactly as possible the various government ministries. This will prevent overlap between committees, and also prevent legislation or policy proposals from falling between the cracks in the oversight referral process. It is also easier for the officials from the government departments concerned to develop good working relationships with the committee membership and staff, and provide a smooth flow of information between the two.

### EXCLUSIVE JURISDICTION

With specific parallel mandates to government ministries, committees can be assured exclusive jurisdiction on issues. Knowing they have the sole mandate to pursue an issue will ensure greater ownership and vigilance.

### MANDATES

Permanent committees require not only mandates that provide exclusive subject matter responsibility to each committee but the powers needed to explore those mandates rigorously. Each committee should have a permanent order of reference to enable it to investigate any matters falling within its area of responsibility. It also requires the power to send for witnesses, hear testimony and table reports. When studying legislation, committees should be given the power to amend it because committees that only advise are far less powerful than committees with the power to make changes.

### INDEPENDENT RESEARCH

The committees should have access to research support that is independent of government. This could be provided through a Parliamentary Library Research Office or by giving each committee a small budget in order to hire independent outside researchers.

### BILL REFERRAL

The stage at which a bill is referred to a committee will govern the ability of the committee to change the bill. Once the legislature has voted on a bill at second reading and thereby approved its principle, the scope for change is narrowed to only that which falls within the approved scope. Referring a bill to committee before the house has pronounced upon it gives that committee the power to make more sweeping changes to the proposed legislation. Adding the provision that governments may at their choice refer bills to committee either before or after the second reading can be useful. Depending upon the executive's commitment to the measure and the available timeframe, it is possible to obtain a much more thorough revision of the proposed legislation and greater public input before the bill is passed into law.

### CLOSED SESSIONS

Those who favour an open democratic process will rarely sanction meetings held behind closed doors. In relation to committee hearings, this normally holds true as well. Not only should they normally meet in open session, the public should be encouraged to attend, and to submit briefs and opinions to the committee on the various issues under study. Occasionally, however, particularly when a committee is drafting a report to the house on a contentious issue, a closed-door meeting may allow for the trade-offs and compromises that may be required to produce a unanimous report, which might simply not be possible to achieve in a public meeting.

The scope for enhancing the effectiveness of legislatures extends considerably beyond committee reform, as evidenced by the further possibilities outlined below.

### Agenda control

A legislature with the power to determine its own agenda will have a much greater capacity to influence outcomes than one where the government alone decides the agenda. Among Western legislatures, the Dutch, the Italian and the US legislatures all decide their agenda independently from the executive. The United Kingdom Parliament has little capacity to set its own agenda. A legislature with little or no power to decide what business will be debated can have very little control over a powerful executive. One of the basic questions about the relevance of parliament can be raised when debating this point.

### Party discipline

One of the most common reasons cited by members of parliaments in many countries for their lack of a meaningful role relates to the high level of party discipline to which they are subjected. Members who are consistently bound by party solidarity to vote with their party on every issue, regardless of their personal views or the wishes of their constituents, will often feel totally powerless. The Honourable Peter Lougheed, who was for many years the Premier of the Province of Alberta, Canada, spoke recently at the Public Policy Forum in Toronto. In discussing the need to make Parliament more relevant, he said his one regret as Premier was not allowing more free votes in the Alberta legislature. He now feels that by allowing members to decide more issues without the party whips imposing the decision on them 'would restore the stature and the relevance of the individual member'.

### Resources

One of the major requirements of elected members to enable them to adequately represent their constituents, to play a meaningful role in the legislature, and to be active and productive committee members, is adequate resources. They need access to both secretarial services and research support if they are to fulfil their many functions in an effective manner, and such resources must be independent of government for all members regardless of party. They also need offices, telephones and information technology equipment, particularly access to the Internet, as a research tool and as a means of communicating with constituents.

In the past the role of an elected member was something that could be done on a part-time basis, because many legislatures only sat for a few months a year in total or a few hours per day. Increasingly, however, there are fewer and fewer parliaments in the world where it is possible for a member to continue another job in addition to being an elected member. Suitable salaries and allowances are required to enable members to devote themselves full-time to their elected role.

In large, busy legislatures, not only must members work full-time for long hours just to try to keep up with the workload, but they also need adequate support staff to assist them. Dealing with constituency issues, attending caucus meetings, being an active member on a couple of committees, attending debates and question time in the house, preparing speeches, doing research on issues: the list of items a member must be involved in is virtually endless. In order to do justice to a demanding job, elected members must be supported adequately.

### Communication with the electorate

Enabling the public to interact more easily and frequently with elected members and with parliamentary committees is an important and useful adjunct to the legislative function. Elected members are the interface between the voter and the government, and can provide the executive with needed information on the current concerns and problems of the public. Having a responsive parliament, where voters' views are important and public input is valued, would go a long way to alleviating the cynicism many members of the public now feel toward politicians.

There is widespread criticism of the levels of apathy among citizens of many countries in relation to politics, and among young people in particular. This is reflected in low voter turnout at elections, small numbers of people joining political parties and running for election, and low participation in political events. Even reading political news in newspapers has fallen significantly in the past fifteen years in some countries, according to a recent study from the Montreal-based Institute for Research in Public Policy, by Henry Milner, a political scientist at Laval

University. In his study of eighteen industrialised countries he found that newspaper readership and adult illiteracy rates are the best predictors of political knowledge among citizens. The Scandinavian countries scored the highest and have the highest voter participation.

Apathy in relation to politics can result from lack of understanding of what a strong democratic legislature can accomplish, and may lead to people taking the law into their own hands. When violence occurs or vigilante justice is meted out rather than people relying on existing systems and structures, how often is that due to people taking action because they feel there is no alternative? Apathy in relation to the political process and animosity to parliament can be a dangerous thing. Parliaments are the link between the people and the executive. They need to reach out and bring civic responsibility to people. One only need talk to someone from a country recently deprived of democratic government to understand how precious and fragile it is; how it must constantly be guarded and nourished. Reforming and strengthening parliaments will go a long way to restoring public confidence in their elected politicians.

### Transparency and effectiveness

In addition, the conflict between transparency and effectiveness is one that must be considered more carefully and understood more widely. Legislatures and their committees must meet openly. The public must not only be able to attend but also encouraged to listen, through the widespread coverage of debates, and participate in the dialogue. Members need to communicate regularly with constituents by using the Internet and websites, by travelling in their constituencies, holding regular meetings and visiting schools. Committees need to seek public input into their deliberations. Interaction and frequent exchanges of ideas will help to break down the public cynicism and apathy that currently exists in many parts of the world. Parliament must be open to the people. It must be seen to be relevant to all citizens.

With that in mind, however, there are occasionally times when openness will prevent compromise. When positions have been stated publicly on issues, backing down can be seen as weakness. Saving face is easier when solutions can be reached in private on these occasions. When committees have heard all the evidence and are drafting their final report on a contentious issue, it is far easier to arrive at a compromise solution behind closed doors. With give and take, it is possible to reach unanimity. The final report will then send a far stronger message, and will achieve more in the long run. Closed doors occasionally make sense.

Lord Norton is of the view that all proceedings in parliament should be public, and he does not agree therefore with any deviations from that rule. However, one specific example in which a departure from complete transparency has proven useful in the Canadian house is the election of the speaker. By means of a secret ballot, elected members vote for a speaker. The process is held in public, the ballot is secret. Were the vote to be public, party solidarity would likely prevail. The prime minister's choice would invariably get the nod assuming the government had a majority. That choice might not present the house with the candidate best able to work well with government, backbenchers and the opposition. A speaker elected by secret ballot, by all members of the house, undertakes the difficult job from a solid base, knowing he or she has the support of the majority of the house. The clerk of the house counts the ballots behind closed doors, and the winner is announced in the chamber. No totals are ever revealed and the ballots are immediately destroyed to protect the secrecy. The secret ballot in this instance has proven to be a very good initiative, which has helped to strengthen the independence of the speakership and the independence of the legislature as a result.

### Conclusion

Strengthening the role of parliaments is not an easy task but it is a crucial one. Democracy is dependent upon a strong legislature to hold the government accountable, to oversee the governing process and to ensure public input into government. Ensuring that legislatures are sufficiently effective to fulfil these vitally important roles requires constant attention and ceaseless constructive effort.

# 6 Do unicameral or bicameral parliaments function more effectively?

*This section is based upon a paper presented by Mr Arthur Donahoe, Secretary–General, Commonwealth Parliamentary Association and on the ensuing plenary discussion.*

In discussing legislative systems, which works best – unicameral or bicameral? The only answer to that question is that it depends. There are staunch advocates on both sides of the question, and strong arguments can be made for either.

### Efficiency

Those in favour of unicameral legislatures point out that it is a faster and more efficient system, which saves both time and money. Taxpayers are seldom keen on paying for salaries, office space, support services, travel, accommodation and so forth, for any more politicians than necessary. A unicameral government will logically have fewer members than two houses would require. Legislation will be enacted more quickly, as it will not have to pass through two houses with the inherent possibilities of conflicts, amendments, negotiation and delay. It cannot help but cost less.

### Accountability

Many argue there is greater accountability with only one house. The other place cannot be blamed for whatever error or omission the disgruntled public wishes to take issue with. Those who favour bicameral systems will say, yes, legislation can be passed more quickly in a unicameral parliament; in fact, too quickly. There is often no time for public awareness to be raised and successful lobbying against certain measures to convince a government to amend or delay the measure. Sober second thought does not happen, and as a result flawed or unpopular legislation sometimes results.

### Diversity

Another strong reason put forward for bicameralism is that a second chamber allows for the rights of diverse groups or regions to be recognised formally. These may be different ethnic groups, regional interests, religious, class, cultural or linguistic differences. The United Nations currently has a policy of promoting bicameralism in countries where racial tensions have been the cause of internal problems, the rationale being that a second chamber can provide a means to try to ease such difficulties. In a diverse country a second chamber can be a safety valve, a place for minority views to be aired. It builds into the system an additional possibility for discussion, consultation and compromise.

Advocates of unicameral legislatures will suggest this is also possible in a single legislature, particularly with proportional representation, which encourages more diversity in representation by its very nature.

### Detailed scrutiny

It is suggested that the members of second chambers, particularly those who are elected for longer periods of time than the lower house, say six years as opposed to three or four, or where some or all members are appointed, have greater time and opportunity to develop expertise in specific subject areas. Fact-finding and subject-matter enquiries carried out by committees of a second chamber are often noted for having more breadth and depth than those of a single chamber, where getting through the business of the day and representing constituents can be all-consuming roles for members.

More detailed scrutiny of legislation is also possible when there is the luxury of more time, and without constituents to represent, which is often true for members in an upper house. This can serve as an added check on the executive.

On the other side of the discussion some would state that in a large unicameral house, committee work will often be a valuable and useful role for those members who are not part of the executive and do not have a specific role in their political party or as a house officer. For many members committee work is a useful balance to constituency business, and they would defend the reports their committees produces as being every bit as valuable as those of upper houses.


### Electoral results ignored

One of the criticisms of a second chamber, where some or all of the members are appointed, is the practice of naming as members those defeated in the lower house. This seems to be a widespread practice, particularly in the Caribbean. The practice is even more widely criticised when such appointed members are then named to the cabinet. The reasoning behind allowing defeated members into the cabinet, by the back door so to speak, is that in small countries, where the population base of experienced political leadership is limited, every possible resource needs to be used. There are, none the less, many vocal detractors, in a democracy, of a process over which the public at large has no control.


### Factors

Quite clearly, there are good reasons for both unicameral and bicameral systems. Each country must choose for itself based on its particular priorities and interests. Does the country have a federal or unitary system? Does it have a large population or small? Is it a vast geographic area spread over several time zones or a small land area where distances are short and easily covered? Is the country composed of a large number of tribes, racial or ethnic groups? Are there many religions and cultures represented? Is cost an important factor? Are there already many layers of local and regional government? What are the problems with the current situation and what is working well? Is there a significant demand for major change such as abolishing or adding a second chamber, or would modifying the existing system suffice to remedy current discontent?

### Revealed preferences

How have countries chosen parliamentary systems? What is the mix of unicameral and bicameral parliaments in the world today? Let us consider the situation in the fifty-three national Commonwealth parliaments. To arrive at fifty-three Pakistan and Fiji are included, even though they are not currently participating in Commonwealth Parliamentary Association activities, and Nigeria is also included, though it is virtually a congressional system. Of these fifty-three parliaments, twenty-one, or roughly 40 per cent, are bicameral. For the total 171 CPA branches the percentage drops to about 19 per cent, because to the twenty-one national bicameral parliaments we only add eleven, those being five Australian states, five Indian states and the Isle of Man. The choice made by slightly less than half of all Commonwealth national parliaments is for a bicameral system, while for the vast majority of provincial, state or territorial legislatures it is unicameral.

Based then on statistics alone, one could say that in parliamentary systems the question is wide open in relation to national parliaments but clearly in favour of unicameral houses for state, provincial and territorial legislatures. The list of national parliaments with bicameral legislatures includes most of the large Commonwealth countries: Australia, Canada, India, Malaysia, Nigeria, Pakistan, South Africa and the United Kingdom. It also includes several mid-sized countries – Jamaica, Namibia, Trinidad and Tobago, Botswana, Lesotho and Swaziland – and several small countries: Antigua and Barbuda, the Bahamas, Barbados, Belize, Fiji, Grenada and Saint Lucia.

How are members chosen in second chambers in the various Commonwealth parliaments and how do the powers of such chambers vary?

## Upper houses

### Australia

In the federal parliament in Australia, both the House of Representatives and the Senate are elected. Because of this the upper house in Australia is a powerful body, which can and does exercise its powers regularly. It has blocked important government legislation, refused to vote supply and forced elections. Where the majority party in one house differs from the majority in the other, votes along party lines can make it difficult for the government of the day to get its legislative programme passed, and the colour and language of Australian politics can be exciting to watch.

### India

In India the Rajya Sabha or upper house is largely composed of members chosen by the elected members of the state or territorial assemblies. Impasses between the upper and lower house are dealt with by means of a joint sitting where the numeric superiority of the lower house can usually carry the vote.

### South Africa

In South Africa, Parliament consists of two houses: the National Assembly, which is elected for a term of five years and consists of no fewer than 350 and no more than 400 members, and the National Council of Provinces (NCOP).

The NCOP replaced the former Senate, which had been judged too party political and ineffective, and came into operation on 4 February 1997. The rationale behind the NCOP was to integrate the concept of a unitary state with the existence of nine provincial governments by ensuring that provincial interests are taken into account in the national sphere of government. It does this mainly by providing a national forum for public consideration of issues affecting the provinces.

The NCOP is presided over by a chairperson assisted by two deputy chairpersons. The current Chairperson is Ms Naledi Pandor, a regional representative of the CPA Executive Committee. There are ninety delegates in the NCOP. Each of the nine provinces has a single delegation consisting of four special and six permanent delegates which is headed by the premier of each province (or his/her nominee). The delegation must reflect the strength of the different parties in the province. In addition to the nine delegations, ten representatives from local government also participate in the NCOP but do not have the right to vote.

Bills that relate to national functions and do not directly affect the provinces, such as defence and foreign affairs, are still considered by the NCOP. Each delegate has one vote, but the National Assembly can accept or reject any changes put forward. However, when a bill is deemed to affect provinces the process is different. Each province has one vote and if there is no agreement between the NCOP and the National Assembly the matter is sent to a mediation committee (which is composed of nine members of the NCOP and nine members of the National Assembly). In the event of agreement both houses must then vote on the bill, but if mediation is unsuccessful the National Assembly can override the NCOP with a two-thirds majority. However, at least six of the nine provinces in the NCOP must agree to any amendment of the Constitution.

Delegates on the NCOP represent the legislature in each province and not the individual voters directly, and it therefore follows the practice of the Council of States or Rajya Sabha in India rather than the directly elected Australian Senate.

### United Kingdom

Britain, of course, has recently made significant changes to the House of Lords, reducing the number of hereditary peers to less than 100 and setting up an Appointments Commission to nominate independent members to the Lords and to vet all nominations to life peerages. The changes to this upper house are ongoing at the present time and will, no doubt, bear watching. The House of Lords has the power to veto legislation but this merely suspends a bill. Ultimately the Commons will prevail and the bill will receive Royal Assent.

### Barbados

In Barbados the Senate also has a veto power over legislation. There, the lower house must approve a bill in two successive parliamentary sessions to overcome the Senate veto and enable the bill to receive assent by the head of state.

### Jamaica

In Jamaica, Senate opposition to legislation can be overcome by passing the bill three times with an absolute majority in the lower house. This applies to all but constitutional matters.

### Botswana

Botswana is an interesting variant on the more usual makeup of an upper and lower house. The National Assembly has forty-six seats of which forty are directly elected. The president is then elected by the Assembly and receives a seat, and he may appoint four additional seats. The Assembly also votes for a speaker who need not be an elected member. He or she is also given a seat. The House of Chiefs has fifteen members of whom eight represent the eight largest tribes and four are elected at large from the smaller tribes. These twelve then elect the three remaining members. The National

Assembly deals with most of the legislation by itself, but must consult the House of Chiefs on any constitutional changes and on all tribal matters; for example issues dealing with tribal or property matters or marriage rites.

### Canada

Canada is a good example of the norm as regards a Commonwealth parliament in that the national Parliament is bicameral while the ten provinces and three territories are unicameral. Such was not always the case. Five of the ten provinces had appointed upper houses when they joined the Confederation. All were subsequently abolished: Manitoba in 1876, New Brunswick in 1892, Prince Edward Island in 1893, Nova Scotia in 1928 and Quebec in 1968.

### Case study: Nova Scotia

The abolition of the appointed upper house in Nova Scotia, after more than sixty years of existence, is an interesting case study of just how difficult it can be to change parliamentary institutions, even when a strong will to do so exists.

According to Professor Murray Beck in his book *The Government of Nova Scotia*, the elected lower house or Assembly considered the appointed upper house or Council to be redundant, and held that view consistently from 1878 on. Being able to do something about it was a different matter. Up until 1928 efforts at abolition were made on a continuing basis. When vacancies arose they were left unfilled. Individuals who supported abolition were appointed to the Council on the understanding they would vote accordingly when a bill was before them. However, when the time came to vote themselves out of office some of the councillors had changes of heart, and constitutional arguments were made against abolition. The possibility of joint action with the other two maritime provinces, who were also proceeding with abolition, was explored, but to no avail. Recourse was even made to seeking permission from the British government to appoint sufficient extra councillors to enable an abolition vote to carry. The British Parliament was also asked to consider amending the Canadian Constitution to abolish the upper house.

The single successful change to the Council during this long period was a statute that reduced the appointed period for councillors from life to a term of ten years.

In 1925 a Conservative government was elected which had campaigned on the promise of abolition. There was but a single Conservative councillor in the upper house, the Liberals having been in power for the previous forty years, so the way was clear for concerted action. Tentative offers of pensions were made to councillors in the event of abolition. These were rejected. The Lieutenant Governor was asked to appoint sufficient extra councillors to enable an abolition vote to carry. The Governor-in-Council, when consulted, suggested a legal determination be made to assure that he indeed had the power to appoint extra members.

In 1927, the Judicial Committee of the Privy Council at Westminster, then Canada's highest Court of Appeal, ruled first, that indeed the Lieutenant Governor in Council did have the right to appoint an unlimited number of councillors, and second, that all councillors appointed prior to the 1925 Statute amendment were appointed during pleasure. The Lieutenant Governor in Council, that is the government of the day, could decide at any time when that pleasure ceased, and did. Accordingly, with the subsequent vacated seats and newly appointed abolitionist councillors, the 1928 bill to bring the Council to its demise was duly passed by both houses, and the Legislative Council of Nova Scotia was no more.

### Canadian situation

The national Parliament in Canada is bicameral. It can be argued that this was an essential condition to Confederation taking place at all. In 1867 the founding provinces agreed to representation in the House of Commons being elected proportional to population only on the condition that a Senate be created with representation on a regional basis.

There were at Confederation twenty-four senators from Ontario, twenty-four from Quebec, and twenty-four from the Maritimes. As the country grew, other provinces and territories were added with virtually the same representation in the Senate. By 1915 there were twenty-four senators from western Canada, composed of six each from the four western provinces. When Newfoundland joined in 1949 it was also given six Senate seats. Each of the three territories now has one senator for a total of 105. All senators are nominated by the sitting prime minister and serve until they reach the age of 75.

It was originally envisaged that the Senate would represent the regions of the country and also the cultural diversity. Quebec in particular wanted to protect its language and culture from assimilation into the larger majority. The concept of an appointed Senate, a chamber of sober second thought, was also part of the original intent, to balance any radical tendencies of the elected House of Commons. The Senate's approval was required for all legislation, and with the exception of money bills any legislation could be introduced in the Senate.

For almost the last 100 years there has been talk of Senate reform, everything from total abolition, to making it elected, to massive changes in its role and function. Calls for reform seem to reach a peak in times of economic restraint, when the Senate is widely criticised as being redundant, an unnecessary duplication and a waste of money. The need for change is also a major issue when the political majority in the House of Commons and the Senate differ and there are the inevitable conflicts between the two chambers. When times are good and disputes minimal, little discussion of Senate reform or abolition is heard.

There is a specific division of powers in the Canadian Constitution, with the provinces and territories each having their own elected legislature, where there exists a strong voice for regional interests. These legislatures are also, of course, primarily responsible for issues like education and health care delivery, where language and culture play a role in public demands.

The Senate in Canada, it can be argued, is less active in defending regional interests than was originally envisaged. This is because it has tended to have a majority of its members from the same political party as the lower house and because the provincial governments have always had a strong and often united voice in federal–provincial relations. Another serious impediment to Senate reform has been the requirement for provincial agreement, and it is rare for the provinces to agree with the federal government on constitutional issues.

In summary then, the Canadian situation of unicameral provinces and territories and a bicameral national legislature is unlikely to change any time soon.

# 7 Information technology and parliamentary effectiveness

*This section follows from presentations by Senator Dato'Hasbullah Ghazi Bin Ramli, Parliament of Malaysia, and Sandy Lee, Member of the Legislative Assembly of the Northwest Territories, Canada, and the subsequent discussions which ensued.*

Information technology is a tool that has the potential for enhancing both the ease of accessing information about parliament and the volume of material that can be made widely available. It also has considerable potential for improving communication between elected representatives and the public.

By expanding the use of information communication technology (ICT), the electorate can access more information about parliament and parliamentary business. With more facts obtained more easily and quickly, they will be better able to assess what is going on, form opinions and make decisions. ICT helps everyone to share knowledge and better understand problems and issues.

The public can more easily become participants in the political process, whether by learning and understanding more about what is going on, or by communicating electronically with their elected representatives, or by sharing their views and opinions electronically with a committee. ICT is a powerful tool that opens doors to a multitude of enhancements to the democratic process. It cannot be overlooked.

Some of the most popular and rapidly growing forms of ICT such as the Internet, e-mail, chat-groups, newsgroups, e-learning and videoconferencing, can all be used, and are being used by various legislatures throughout the world. They are able to more easily involve people in the parliamentary process and elected members can do their jobs better.

### Keeping pace with the public

Technology in legislatures does however need to keep pace with society as a whole, and should neither lead society nor lag too much behind. There is little point in spending large amounts of money to provide extensive databases of information about the functioning of a parliament, if the majority of the electorate do not have computers with hook-ups to the Internet. Conversely, if libraries, schools, and the general public are widely using computers, legislatures must meet the demands for online information about what they are doing and provide the means for interactive communication between the elected members and the public. Whatever the current situation in a particular country, demand will grow overnight as the costs for equipment continue to decrease over time and access to the Internet becomes more widely affordable and accessible. Legislatures must be planning ahead of demand in order to be ready and able to meet expectations as they continue to rise.

The spectrum of technology use in the various legislatures throughout the world is enormous, and this is clearly an area where one size does not fit all. It must also be stated clearly from the outset that a low level or even total lack of technology in no way relates to either inefficiency or inability to provide effective, well-run democratic government. Technology is only a tool to enhance, not a basic requirement. Where resources permit however, it can provide tremendous advantages for improving the operations of a parliament and for increasing its effectiveness.

## Bridging the digital gap

Every legislature should be addressing the issue of ICT no matter what its current state of involvement. While such technology is available everywhere in the world, its usage varies widely not only from country to country, but within countries. The 'digital gap' exists everywhere. To address discrepancies an agenda is required, first to assess the options and possibilities and then to rank the possibilities in order of priority. Without a plan, nothing will get done and the gap will merely widen. Everyone must make choices and decide which options are more important for them. With a good agenda not only will progress be made by the choices selected but also all will fit together and interrelate, each building upon the other. The question then becomes, what are the possibilities that ICT offers to parliaments and legislators?

First, parliament itself will be producing information every day it sits that will be of interest to a wide variety of users. The media and the public want to see, hear and read about the debates that take place in the chamber and in committee. Only a few people live close enough and have the time available to attend the public galleries and actually be present during a sitting. Most citizens depend on the media to provide commentary on the issues being debated in the legislature. In many cases the public is able, however, to view televised proceedings or listen to radio broadcasts, and they do so in surprisingly large numbers.

## Broadcasting proceedings

I recall a trip in a taxi in a developing country during which the driver was listening intently to a radio broadcast of a political debate. When I asked him about it, he said their parliamentary debates were always interesting and important to follow and were regularly carried on the radio. He and his friends always listened in and discussed what went on.

In Canada, the House of Commons in Ottawa is broadcast live on cable television throughout the country, and has been since

1977. Letters and phone calls from viewers over a lengthy period reveal that a surprisingly large number of Canadians both regularly follow debates and are keenly interested in what is going on, phoning and writing with questions. I remember a letter from a young mother who was home from work for the first time during the day with her new baby. She wrote that initially she had turned on the Parliamentary Channel for something to watch while feeding her infant son. She had now become a 'political junkie' hooked on her daily dose of Question Period, and was already preparing to tape it when she returned to work so as not to miss anything. Perhaps it harks back to the adage, 'If you build it they will come'. On the other side of the coin, it is hard to fault the public for not paying attention to what goes on in their legislature if they are far removed and have no ready access.

The interest in what is going on in parliament will certainly vary depending on what is being debated, but those working in legislatures that have televised proceedings or radio coverage know that there is a consistent group of observers. For major items, such as budget presentations and throne speeches, the size of the audience can be quite large.

Bringing parliament to the people is something that the use of television and radio broadcasting makes easier and more convenient. In a country with a large geographic area like Canada, where travel is time-consuming and expensive, it is a particularly useful technological tool.

As well as its being broadcast live or time-delayed on regular television or radio channels, it is also possible to provide live or delayed audio and video coverage over the Internet. This has cost advantages over regular broadcasting and will provide for even wider access. It is an area that is increasingly being used by provincial and state legislatures in North America.

### E-Hansard

Most legislatures produce a Hansard or verbatim text record of their debates. In the past this was always produced in printed form only. Printing, binding and shipping voluminous texts could be costly, and the material when finally received would often be quite dated. Putting the Hansard record on the Internet will not only save these printing costs but will also allow access throughout the world to the debates, often the next day. Material can also be made more easily available in a variety of languages, a major advantage in many countries.

## E-bills

The text of bills that are being debated in legislatures and committee proceedings can also be made available in this way, vastly improving accessibility in a timely fashion to information for which there is usually a high demand. Anyone who wants a hard copy (on paper) only needs to download the text and print it for him or herself. The cost savings in the Canadian house of putting Hansard on line, rather than printing it, was in the millions of dollars annually, not to mention the number of trees that were saved by reducing printing.

## Parliamentary websites

Many legislatures now have websites where they provide access not only to this kind of regular information about their proceedings but also historical background material, lists of elected members with their biographies and addresses, schedules of upcoming meetings, and various other useful information about the parliament. There are often links to other related websites such as to those of each individual elected member and to the various political parties, parliamentary associations and government departments.

As a large number of legislatures throughout the world now have websites, finding information about what is currently happening in other provinces, states or countries is now easier and faster than it ever was before. As well as other parliaments, most international parliamentary organisations such as the Commonwealth

Parliamentary Association and the Inter Parliamentary Union now have websites with online information about the work they do, as well as material they have compiled on topics of interest and data on various countries. They usually list upcoming meetings and conferences as well as publications, which can often be ordered or downloaded immediately. Doing research, gathering information, gaining knowledge about what others have done or are doing in respect of parliaments or electoral systems has never been as convenient and accessible.

The main users of parliamentary websites tend to be libraries, lobbyists and law firms, but schools are increasingly becoming frequent visitors. Educating our young people about how their parliament works is one of the key tasks that most countries are not yet doing well enough. The Internet can be a great resource for this. Being able to provide timely information about what is happening in parliament and how parliament works is an important means of keeping a democratic government accountable and accessible.

The Internet can be a wonderful educational resource, and teachers are widely accessing it as a teaching tool. Information about parliament downloaded from parliamentary websites can provide background and discussion material for civics classes, for example. In parts of the country where personal computer use is low, placing terminals in schools and libraries is one way of opening up their wealth of information to everyone. This has worked well in the far north of Canada, for example. The Internet is an important tool that allows all this to be done in a fast and efficient manner so material is not dated or stale, but always of current interest.

### Parliamentary intranets

Many legislatures now also have intranets. These are internal networks that allow all elected members and their staff, as well as support staff of the institution itself, to be interconnected. They are able to share files, obtain information from various internal data bases, schedule appointments and book meetings, quickly and in a secure manner. Closed intranets are far less susceptible to hackers and other invaders with malicious intent. For this reason, security problems are much less of an issue than when using the Internet.

Intranets can also connect the members' legislative offices with their constituency offices. This allows them access to the same material whether they are in the capital or back in the constituency, which can prevent duplication and save enormous amounts of time and effort.

ICT now means that staying in touch has never been easier for a member. With a portable laptop computer and a cellphone it is now possible for a member to access his or her electronic mailbox from virtually anywhere in the world. When travelling within the constituency, or on committee business within the country, or to international conferences, the member is never out of touch with the office back home. He or she can read mail and send instructions back to staff any time of the day or night. The messages are waiting for them when they sign on to their computers. Speech notes, background information, current news, whatever the member needs, can all be accessed from anywhere.

### Constituency links

Many elected members will now have their own websites allowing them to provide information to their constituents via the Internet about what they are currently involved in, what policies or proposals they are advocating, when and where their next public meeting will be held, and so forth. The public can also send mail electronically to their members through the Internet and get an electronic message back.

Where before constituents might have mailed a letter and waited several weeks for a response, they now send an e-mail and expect a reply within a day or two. This can be both a benefit to the constituent, and a problem for the member. In the past a member might have had the luxury of several days to assemble a response to a request from a constituent. Now with e-mail the sender expects a quick response. The volume of correspondence has also increased enormously, for it is far easier to prepare a short message and send it with the click of a button than it was to sit down and write and then mail a letter. Both the volume increase and the faster turnaround requirement have contributed to demands by members for more resources to handle the increased workload. Cutbacks in the number of elected members in some legislatures in recent years have only made this problem worse.

### The public pulse

When parliaments are dealing with contentious issues, various action groups will sometimes coordinate campaigns to inundate members with e-mails and letters supporting or opposing such issues. Extremely high volumes of targeted messages have been known to overload the capacity of networks and completely block computer systems. Safeguards need to be put in place to protect against this happening. Members clearly want the public's reaction on various issues, but not at the expense of crashing computer systems.

Opening up parliament to the public has frequently been cited as a current major goal of governments with various legislatures trying many new ways of getting the public more involved. A number of Canadian legislatures have experimented recently with websites for parliamentary committees, set up in order to invite the public to send briefs, letters and opinions to the committee on various topics it is investigating. Some legislatures have experimented with setting up 'chat groups' on various topics, using the Internet to get public reaction to new proposals that are being considered.

### Videoconferencing

Committees are also making increasing use of video teleconferencing. Rather than needing to travel vast distances, with large numbers of staff, at great cost, in order to hold public hearings, witnesses can provide testimony by means of video teleconferencing. Members are able to ask questions of the witnesses and the entire proceedings can be taped. This is one area where technology has improved radically over a short period of time, and costs have also come down a lot since its inception.

### Some caveats

On the negative side, some will say that the face-to-face contact is an important element that is being given up, and that those who live far from the centre of national government may feel even more marginalised by a mere electronic presence. There has to be a balance between increasing the ability to reach out to people and maintaining a continuing physical presence on a regular basis.

Yet another negative aspect of the increase in parliamentary technology, is the growing dependence that comes with it. Where once votes could be taken in a legislature by counting members passing through the lobbies or standing in their places in the chamber – and in many legislatures that is still the practice – many legislatures now have electronic voting, with buttons to push and electronic scoreboards recording the results. Power failures or computer system malfunctions can now stop parliamentary proceedings where before that was never an issue. It does not happen frequently, but it can cause significant difficulties and delays when problems do occur. It is wise to consider incorporating back-up procedures when any such system is installed to guard against this.

Security is another issue, which needs to be carefully thought out and effectively provided for in relation to ICT. Legislators may have access to the very latest technology and the best databases and information networks. But if some computer hacker has deliberately sabotaged the system, or some virus has infected files, there will be major delays and inconveniences until the problems are isolated and fixed. Parliament must be able to continue to operate, particularly in times of crisis, so safeguards and back-ups are crucial. By using passwords and swipe cards given only to those allowed on the system, one can restrict access and provide a reasonable level of security. However carelessness or theft can break down such measures.

Work is advancing on enhanced biometric security devices such as fingerprint scanners and eye retina scanners that will ensure that only authorised people have access to computer networks and particularly sensitive data. Such sophisticated security devices are not inexpensive, which is a major consideration at present.

### Electoral applications

ICT has an increasing role not only for parliaments themselves, but for the holding of elections as well. Electronic technology has greatly facilitated the enormous task of preparing, keeping, updating and accessing voter registries. An accurate, up-to-date list, that can be verified quickly and easily and amended when necessary, is extremely important to the holding of democratic elections. The larger the number of voters, the bigger the task of providing accurate reliable voter lists. ICT can be a great asset here.

Electronic voting machines can also provide a secure, easy to use way for voters to register their choices, and when polling closes, counting and compilation of results can be completed quickly and efficiently.

In Brazil, the introduction of voting machines not only increased electoral participation significantly; it also reduced the number of spoiled votes. When technology simplifies voter registration, increases participation at the polls and provides more timely and accurate results, the high cost can often be justified.

In holding elections, security is of course a significant concern. It is necessary to prevent fraud or manipulation of results and a recorded back-up of an electronic system is essential to allow for recounts and verifications when complaints arise. When any new system is to be introduced, it is essential to spend the time necessary to survey carefully the various systems available and see them in operation. Not every system works the same way, and choices and cost will vary considerably depending upon specific needs. The computer system should not drive the process, but rather one should be able to find a system that fits the needs with little or no modifications. Once it has been chosen, sufficient lead-time is required for delivery, testing, and training for the staff who will operate the system. Dry runs and practice sessions are also important. The public also needs to be educated before the election as to how the new system will work, and what they can expect when they come to register their vote. Careful planning will ensure a smooth transition from one way of voting to another.

### Looking ahead

ICT can transform the way elections are carried out, the way parliaments work, the way members represent their constituents, and the way the public interacts with the legislature. Democracy can be enhanced by the use of technology to boost public participation and involvement. More information can be shared with a larger number of people in a shorter period of time. ICT has a high cost, but if it helps in a significant way to open parliament up to the people, most will agree it is a cost worth paying.

# PART III

ELECTORAL SYSTEMS
AND PROCESSES

# 8 Alternative electoral systems

*This chapter is based upon a paper presented by Mr Anders Johnsson, Secretary–General of the Inter-Parliamentary Union and the ensuing discussion and by a paper presented by Baroness Diana Maddock, House of Lords, UK, and the ensuing discussion.*

Regular elections, where the will of the people can be tested fairly and the population can choose freely who is to govern them, are an essential element of democratic government. Putting an electoral system in place and holding elections regularly requires decisions to be made on many questions, most of which should continue to be asked as circumstances change and as a country evolves and matures.

### The right to vote

To the question who should have the right to vote, the easy answer is that universal suffrage is a requirement for democracy. In a situation where the vote is denied because of gender, race, colour or religion, most would agree that such a situation was undemocratic. Kuwait, for example, denies the vote to women. If half a population is disenfranchised, it is difficult to argue the situation is democratic.

Having stated the obvious, most countries do impose some minor restrictions on who may vote. For example, most countries require a person to be the legal age of majority in order to vote. In other words, an elector must be old enough to make an informed, independent judgement. Many countries will deny the vote for mental incompetence, or to those in prison. Some countries deny the vote to certain high officials such as judges or electoral officers, in order to avoid potential criticisms of political bias. Residency requirements are another common restriction, the assumption being that a non-resident is less knowledgeable about current issues and candidates. In some jurisdictions, there is a link between representation and the obligation to pay taxes. While restrictions vary widely from country to country, most impose some minor limitations. In all cases, only a very small number of people should be disenfranchised, and for justifiable reasons.

### The right to be elected

Who should have the right to be elected? Ideally everyone who can vote should be able to stand for office. However, because the purpose of an election it to choose representatives to sit in an assembly and make decisions on the affairs of state, most countries impose some restrictions here as well. Qualifications may relate to nationality, place of residence, age, personal conduct, ability and so forth.

### Alternative models

Having discussed who can stand for office and who can vote, the next obvious question is how elections will be run. In choosing an electoral system many factors influence the decision: everything from cultural background, political experience, societal values, cost, need for simplicity, desire to be just, to be inclusive or even to be up to date. First, however, one needs to have an understanding of what the different systems are and how they work; their strengths and weaknesses. There are many valuable resource areas and reference works available on this subject, so this chapter will provide on overview only of the three broad types of electoral systems that are in use in the world: the majority system, the proportional system and the mixed system.

*Majority systems (plurality-majority systems)*

The oldest electoral system, the majority system, existed before the advent of political parties, and for a very long time it was the only electoral system. Basically, the candidate who receives the majority of the votes cast is declared the winner. There are however, several variations possible within this system depending upon whether it is a single member constituency or multi-member, and even within a single member system, variants exist.

First-past-the-post (FPTP) or a simple majority of votes cast is the commonest variant. Its major advantage is its absolute simplicity. It is easily understood by everyone and straightforward to implement. Every voter is given a ballot with all candidates listed and chooses one, or the voter is given a blank ballot on which he or she writes the name of the preferred candidate. When all votes are counted the candidate with the most votes wins, regardless of the total number of votes cast. With only two candidates, the winner will have 50 per cent plus one or more of the votes cast. With several candidates, the winner might have only a very small percentage of the votes cast, but as long as he or she has more than anyone else, he or she wins.

Detractors of the simple majority system argue that it is not a just practice for someone to be elected with only 20 or 30 per cent of the votes, which can occur when several candidates are running and the vote is split among them all. In its favour, there is no uncertainty as to the results provided the process is fair. In a two-candidate election, if one candidate has 1000 votes and another has 1001, the latter wins.

A variant on the simple majority is the requirement for an absolute majority of the votes cast. In this case a candidate is not elected until he or she has obtained 50 per cent plus one of the votes cast. A second ballot is held if the first has not delivered such a majority. This is usually done several days or a week or two after the first ballot. It can either be a run-off between the top two candidates from the first ballot, where one of them will of necessity be the winner on the second ballot, or a simple majority can be sufficient to win the second round. The requirement for a second round, of course, costs extra time and money and allows for additional campaigning between votes.

Another variant on the majority system is the preferential or alternative voting system. Here the elector chooses one candidate but also indicates, in declining order, his or her preference for the other candidates. If no one wins an absolute majority of the votes cast on the first count, the candidate with the least number of votes is dropped and the votes for second choice on those ballots are added to the totals. This exercise is repeated as many times as necessary to obtain an absolute majority for one candidate, who then becomes the winner.

*Proportional systems*

Many think that proportional representation is a new system, which overcomes all the problems of majority systems. It has, in fact, been in use for over a hundred years. Belgium used it as early as 1889. In addition, it is not without its detractors. Proponents argue that it is a more just system, for the results proportionately reflect the voters' wishes along party lines. Smaller parties, women and minorities are all thought to have better chances of being elected under proportional systems. In principle, no set of political views will be excluded from electoral representation provided it receives sufficient votes.

On the negative side, because the elector is voting for lists of candidates chosen and ordered by the various political parties, the elector is removed from the elected. It is no longer one candidate representing each constituency, where voters know who their member of parliament is. A list of candidates is elected, none of whom may reside in or represent a constituency per se.

Removing an unpopular member is also more difficult for electors in a proportional system, because if the party continues to put the individual's name near the top of its list, its proportional vote share may well ensure re-election.

Another aspect of this system is that it encourages the formation of small parties, as well as parties representing minority groups, single issues and so forth. Such parties have a better chance of having at least some members elected under this kind of system. While this provides a broader base of elected members, it can and often does lead to political fragmentation. Many more parties usually end up being elected. If no one party has sufficient members elected to form a government, then coalitions are required. Proponents argue that this favours consensus and compromise. Opponents say it can lead to political instability and inability to govern.

A proportional system, whatever its faults, ensures that all votes count for something. In fully proportional representation, the whole country is effectively one constituency. Each party presents the elector with a list of candidates long enough to fill every vacancy. The party chooses the candidates and the order in which they appear on the list. In a closed list system, voters choose one list. In an open list system, they choose names from any list, up to the number of vacancies. The votes are tallied and proportionately allocated to each party, which thereby has elected the number of candidates on its list that correspond to that proportion, either from the top down in a closed list, or by name in an open list system.

The problems with the fully proportional system are obvious. In a country with a large number of seats in the assembly, the party lists are very long and those elected are far removed from the voters. A person in the voting booth is faced with books of lists, probably containing many names totally unknown to him or her. In a closed list system, electors vote by party only, with no means to affect which candidates win seats. In an open list system, nationally known figures will likely receive more votes. Sports heroes, entertainers and outspoken advocates on particular issues will probably increase in the legislature - in other words, known names. This no doubt makes for an interesting legislature. How representative it is in governing is another question.

Most countries, rather than having a fully proportional voting system, opt instead for limited proportional representation. The country is divided into various constituencies and the seats are distributed among them. There will of necessity be proportional discrepancies between the number of votes a party obtains and the number of members elected throughout the country, and this distortion varies depending on the number of constituencies, the number of seats and the number of voters. The number of seats allocated to a particular party on the first count is never exactly equivalent to the total number of votes obtained by that party. The remainder, or votes left over for each, must then be taken into account and distributed, until all seats are allocated.

There are a multitude of mathematical formulae and processes for translating votes into seats in proportional systems, and a great deal of information is readily available for those wishing to study this in detail. One aspect common to most countries is an electoral threshold of votes required for a party to be included in the distribution of seats. The Netherlands, for example, requires 0.67 per cent of the votes, while in the German Bundestag and the Polish Sejm it is 5 per cent. In Liechtenstein it is 8 per cent. This arbitrary threshold also results in proportional distortion, but most feel it is necessary in order to reduce the number of very small parties, and thereby increase political stability and decrease the probability of frequent elections due to an inability to govern.

## Mixed systems

Mixed systems vary enormously and have been growing increasingly popular in recent years. Only a few of the multitude of options possible will be listed to give some idea of the variants. While some of the mixed systems favour majority voting, others favour proportional representation and still others effectively apply both.

### MAJORITY-MIXED SYSTEMS

In a single non-transferable vote model, the voter may vote for only one candidate, even though the constituency in which he or she votes has several seats to be filled. Those candidates who receive the most votes win the seats. This system is used in Jordan and Vanuatu.

For the limited voting method, the voter may vote for several candidates, but his or her total votes cast must be less than the total number of seats to be filled in that constituency. Again, the candidates with the most votes win the seats.

The cumulative voting system allows the voter to cast as many votes as there are seats to be filled in the constituency and he or she may choose either to give all votes to one candidate, or to spread them however he or she wishes among the candidates. Again, the candidates with the most votes win the seats.

## MODIFIED PROPORTIONAL MIXED SYSTEMS

The single transferable vote (the Hare system) method allows the voter to vote for only one candidate regardless of the number of seats to be filled, but to also indicate an order of preference for the other candidates. Once a candidate reaches a specified electoral quotient, he or she is declared elected and any additional votes are then redistributed to other candidates on the basis of second choices indicated. The candidate who receives the fewest votes is eliminated, and his or her votes are also reallocated on the basis of second choices. This process continues, if necessary, until all seats are filled.

## COMBINATION MAJORITY VOTING PROPORTIONAL REPRESENTATION SYSTEM (PARALLEL SYSTEM)

Many countries seek to combine both majority voting and proportional representation, either by using one system in the lower house and the other in the upper house, or by combining both in one house, electing some seats by majority voting and other seats by proportional representation.

Germany, for example, has half the seats in the Bundestag elected from single member constituencies through a simple majority vote. The other half of the seats is divided according to population into the various Lander and elected proportionally. Each party prepares closed lists of candidates for each Land. The voter then casts two votes in each election, one for a constituency representative, and one for a party list.

Hungary uses three different voting methods. In 176 single member constituencies, members are chosen using absolute majority voting. For 152 seats in the twenty regional districts it uses proportional representation based on a single quotient. It also uses full proportional representation for fifty-eight seats chosen from national 'compensation' lists nominated by parties. Each voter has two votes, one for a constituency candidate and one for a party list.

Multi-member constituencies may be determined in a majority system by having the voter choose between various party lists, where the list with the most votes wins all the seats in that constituency. This is known as a closed list. Alternatively, a voter is asked to choose candidates from any party lists up to the number of seats available to be filled, and those candidates with the largest number of votes win. This is the open list, multi-member constituency majority vote system, sometimes called the block vote system.

### Choosing between systems

With the plethora of possible electoral systems available, how does a country choose one over another? What factors need to be considered in making the choice, and what is the breakdown of choices that have been made?

Change in political systems is normally a rather slow evolution, the fine-tuning and adjusting of existing systems over long periods of time. Extreme events or widespread significant discontent with the status quo are required for the major change of replacing one system with another. Examples of such extreme events are obvious: the collapse of communism (Eastern Europe), civil wars (Sri Lanka), the death or overthrow of a powerful dictator (Spain), evidence of significant corruption or fraud within the existing system (Italy), or even total exasperation by the population with the existing situation (New Zealand). Whatever the cause, the people themselves usually drive the requirement for change, and the country's intellectual elite and populist leaders suggest and introduce alternatives, eventually finding a solution that satisfies the majority. Normally, things have to get bad enough that the majority of the population encourages and supports either a major shift in the status quo or a fresh start.

In operating any democratic system of government, the electoral process is key to ensuring that the widest possible number of people have a legitimate voice in choosing who will govern them and how. Without an appropriate electoral system, faith in the entire democratic process is questioned. The system must be fair and be seen to be fair.

There are various essential elements to any electoral system. It should provide the maximum possible participation of citizens in order to be truly democratic. All votes should count for something, if possible, and should be as close as possible to equivalent weight. At the same time, the whole point of elections is to choose representatives who together are capable of governing the country, and the system must allow for sufficient stability for that to be possible.

The electoral system should be free from manipulation and abuse. There should be built-in safeguards, which ensure that is the case, and the population at large should be confident of that. The way in which the system works should be understood readily by all who participate in the elections, and a major education initiative is likely to be required for a new system to be introduced.

There needs to be a close link between the electors and the elected. The elected must be accountable to those who have chosen them, and must reasonably reflect the various social and political groups that make up the country.

Neither of the two major systems, majority vote or proportional representation, can guarantee all of the above criteria to an equal degree, so trade-offs have to be made that are acceptable to the majority. What are these?

Advocates of proportional systems argue that the most important criterion of an electoral system is that it returns representatives who fairly reflect the various interests and political views in the country. In other words, the number of votes a party receives on the national level should translate as closely as possible into seats in the legislature. This is most likely to happen with a proportional system.

On the other hand, proponents of majority systems contend that the principal point of an election is to choose representatives who can form a government and provide stable decision making and leadership for the country. Such stability is more likely to be the outcome of majority system elections in their view.

They also argue that majority systems are more easily understood by all electors and normally provide a far closer link between the voter and the elected member than do proportional systems, which often require a voter to choose party lists rather than individual constituency representatives. Even in mixed proportional systems, where some members represent constituencies and some are chosen proportionately, either the constituency representative must represent a very large number of voters, or the size of the legislature must be extremely large, in order to accommodate the two types of members. In a larger forum, each member will of necessity have less voice.

No electoral system will fill all requirements equally. No system is perfect. Choices must be made based on the specific needs, requirements and priorities of the country or region concerned, the priorities of the people who live there, and the particular circumstances at the time.

# 9 Mandatory voting: the pros and cons

*This section is based upon a presentation by Senator the Honourable Robert Ray, Senator for Victoria, Parliament of Australia, and on the associated discussions in workshop and in plenary.*

Countries that have mandatory voting generally believe very strongly that it is essential in order to ensure full participation in the democratic process. Those who have it cannot imagine being without it. Those countries without mandatory voting cannot imagine introducing it, seeing it as an infringement of rights.

### International experience

Only twenty-four countries in the world subscribe to mandatory voting and they are widely dispersed. The list includes, among others, Australia, Belgium, Bolivia, Fiji, Singapore and Turkey. In some cases it is part of their constitution while in others it forms part of the country's electoral law. Over half of these countries impose no penalty for failure to vote, or provide for a variety of exceptions to the requirement.

In Australia, mandatory voting was adopted in the national parliament through legislation in 1924. It had previously been legislated in the State of Queensland in 1915, primarily because of poor voter turnout. Prior to the introduction of compulsory voting the worst turnout of voters federally had been the 1903 election when only 50.3 per cent of registered voters went to the polls. The first election with compulsory voting in 1925 saw 91.4 per cent of enrolled voters voting. For the subsequent thirty-three Federal elections, the average turnout has been 95 per cent and has never been lower than 93 per cent. Currently, a 95–96 per cent turnout is normal.

The Commonwealth Electoral Act 1918, Section 245, deals with compulsory voting. Basically, voting is considered to be the duty of all Australian citizens 18 years of age or older. It is mandatory for all eligible voters to vote, unless they have a 'valid and sufficient reason'.

The electoral commissioner is required after polling day to prepare a list for each division, of the names and addresses of electors who failed to vote. Within three months after polling day, unless the division returning officer is satisfied that the elector was absent from Australia on voting day, was ineligible to vote, is dead or had a valid and sufficient reason for failing to vote, a penalty notice is sent to all names on this list. The penalty notices advise individuals that there is no record of their having voted, that such failure to vote is an offence, and that if they do not wish to have the matter dealt with by the courts, they must either provide a valid and sufficient reason for not voting, provide the specifics of the circumstances of their voting or pay a fine of twenty dollars. Failure to provide adequate justification or to pay the fine will result in the matter ultimately being dealt with by the courts. It could result in a higher fine, or occasionally when someone is objecting to voting on principle, it could ultimately result in a brief gaol sentence. Throughout Australia, there is a social stigma attached to not voting, which is no doubt a greater deterrence to non-compliance than the fine, which is extremely low.

While it has been compulsory since 1924 to attend the polling booth on election day, whether one votes or not is up to the individual, for the ballot, of course, is secret. It should be noted however that the average spoilt ballots amount to only about 2 per cent of the total, and of these probably only about 0.5 per cent represent protest votes, so mandatory voting legislation has proven to be a very effective way to ensure high participation.

In most countries mandatory voting has usually been introduced post dictatorship or war, or following a period of social turmoil, or as the result of unacceptably low voter participation. It has been effective in improving voter turnout from as low as 20 per cent to over 95 per cent, and has also served to improve the maintenance and updating of voter lists.

## Pros

What are the arguments in favour of mandatory voting? The proponents claim that voting is the civic responsibility of all citizens in a democratic country. Everyone has a duty to vote, which is comparable to other duties such as paying taxes or jury duty. What then is the problem with making it compulsory? Social and political cohesion are promoted when everyone has participated, and alienation from the political process is minimised. Citizens develop a sense of ownership of the political and decision-making process, as it is almost totally inclusive. Governments must consider the total electorate in policy formulation and management, because at the next election they will all be casting a vote.

The election can be focused on the issues and choices before the voters rather than concentrating on getting out the vote. The cost of the election is therefore minimised. The influence of interest groups is also minimised, for the population as a whole has voted, not merely those with strong views on particular issues.

Perhaps the strongest argument in favour of compulsory voting is the fact that is ensures maximum turnout. A government that is chosen by all eligible citizens knows that it has a valid mandate to govern. It cannot make excuses that it does not represent a majority, nor can detractors challenge its legitimacy.

Of almost equal importance is the fact that candidates for election and political parties can concentrate on the issues during a campaign and not worry about getting the vote out. This assists in particular those parties with fewer resources, and for that reason can be seen to be fairer.

## Cons

What are the main arguments against mandatory voting? First is the basic claim that it is an infringement on the liberty of citizens and that it is undemocratic. It is principally for this reason that most countries in the world do not subscribe to it. Some argue that the costs associated with maintaining compliance are not justified, and certainly resources must be allocated to preparing lists of those who did not vote, contacting them, determining whether or not they had valid and sufficient reasons for not voting, and possible court action. Others claim that the potential penalties imposed for non-compliance, which may in some cases involve gaol sentences, far exceed the offence, which is the mere act of not voting in an election.

On the question of basic freedoms and liberties, that is clearly an issue that must be weighed against the collective good, the benefits accruing from total participation in the electoral process.

If we look at voter turnout in countries without compulsory voting, it can vary widely. We recently watched long lines of voters in Sierra Leone standing in the hot sun for their turn to vote in spite of gunfire in the distance. Who can forget the televised news coverage of the 1994 election in South Africa, where the sheer numbers of people waiting patiently for their turn to cast their vote were such an inspiration to the rest of the world? When the struggle for a democratic government, which includes all people, has finally become a reality, the act of casting a vote becomes one of enormous significance. Is there a need to institute compulsory voting laws when people regard the right to vote as something so precious?

In some mid-term congressional elections in the United States the turnout averaged 38 per cent. Whether that low turnout is due to apathy or resignation, or some other cause, the result should cause warning bells to go off. On the one hand something should be done; on the other hand, would such a society accept mandatory voting with equanimity?

One way of dealing with low voter turnout is to consider changing the day of the week chosen for voting or the time polls are open. Sunday for example has been suggested as a more sensible day for voting in the United States, when people would have a little more free time. Such a change would, however, be a very sensitive issue.

## Conclusion

Where it already exists, mandatory voting has a great deal to commend it. In countries where it does not currently exist, introducing it would be extremely difficult in most cases because of the perceived threat to civil liberties. Other measures to increase voter participation would likely meet with wider interest and greater acceptance.

# 10 Gender equality and electoral systems

*This section is based on a paper presented by Dr Lesley Clark, Member of the Legislative Assembly, Queensland, Australia, and on the subsequent plenary discussions.*

In order to have a truly democratic system of government, men and women should be able to work together in all facets of the governance structure, to ensure full participation in decision making. Electoral systems can influence the extent to which this goal is attained.

## Principles

The Inter-Parliamentary Union in its 1977 Declaration of Democracy stated:

> The achievement of democracy presupposes a genuine partnership between men and women in the conduct of the affairs of society in which they work in equality and complementarity, drawing mutual enrichment from their differences.

The Commonwealth Heads of Government, in the 1991 Harare Declaration, adopted a number of items that were agreed to as priority areas for the Commonwealth, including:

> equality for women so that they may exercise their full and equal rights.

The 1994 Inter-Parliamentary Union Plan of Action was inspired by this vision of democracy:

> The concept of democracy will only assume true and dynamic significance when political policies and national legislation are decided upon jointly by men and women with equitable regard for the interests and aptitudes of both halves of the population.

The Beijing Parliamentary Declaration, delivered at the Fourth World Conference on Women held in Beijing in 1995, endorsed the Inter-Parliamentary Union Plan of Action to address the imbalance of participation in political life between men and women. It was also agreed at this conference that women need full and equal access to training and education, with particular attention in many parts of the world to basic literacy. Close to one billion of the world's population is illiterate. Nearly two-thirds of that billion, however, are women and the gap continues to grow, in part due to demographics.

In 1997, the Commonwealth heads of government unanimously agreed to setting a target of no less than 30 per cent women to be full participants in the political, public and private sectors by the year 2005. The recurring theme expressed throughout this conference was the need for an increase in the involvement of women in national decision-making positions in the Commonwealth and throughout the world.

### Women in parliaments

The number of women in parliaments throughout the world was 10.9 per cent in 1975. It increased slowly from 1977, reaching 14.8 per cent in 1988, but by 1995 had dropped back to 11.6 per cent. This was virtually the same as it had been twenty years previously. Thirty per cent is felt by most to be critical mass, that is, the level at which women start to have a significant impact and meaningful input. Fifty per cent would, of course, represent fair gender equity, and it is difficult to talk about fairness in relation to religious, ethnic, cultural or minority groups and not also consider the situation of women.

If there is now widespread support for the inclusion of women, as demonstrated in the positive statements consistently being internationally endorsed, what course of action is required to change the rhetoric into results?

### The link to electoral systems

Some believe that the first-past-the-post system, inherited with the Westminster model of parliament by many countries throughout the world, has been a negative influence on augmenting gender equality in legislatures. The argument is that a proportional representation system would result in more women in legislatures because it is intrinsically more inclusive. Does this argument translate into fact? If we look at a large number of countries and compare those with plurality-majority systems to those with proportional systems, what results do we get?

The data that will be referred to are taken primarily from material compiled by the Inter-Parliamentary Union, see in particular *Women in Parliaments*. This is a database compiled by the IPU on the basis of information provided by the national parliaments of 179 countries, and it is updated regularly. The bibliographic database *Women in Politics* was also consulted, and it is also prepared and regularly updated by the IPU.

In addition, the International Institute for Democracy and Electoral Assistance (IDEA), established in Sweden in 1995 with the aim of promoting and advancing sustainable democracy, has produced a handbook entitled *Women in Parliament: Beyond Numbers*. Published in 1998, this document examines strategies and mechanisms that have increased the impact of women in parliaments around the world, and looks at various means by which women can increase their representation in parliament. Material in this handbook was also helpful in preparing this section.

Taking only those countries with the highest and lowest percentage of women in parliament, what do we find? Nine countries in the world have elected 30 per cent or more women to their legislatures. These are Sweden, Denmark, Finland, Norway, Netherlands, Iceland, Mozambique, Germany and New Zealand. The first seven of those countries have list proportional representation. Germany and New Zealand have mixed member proportional systems. Therefore, all nine countries with 30 per cent or more elected women in their legislatures have either full proportional representation (PR) or a form of PR.

If we now look at the countries that have less than 5 per cent women in their legislatures, there are thirty-four countries in total in this group. These countries are mostly from Africa, the Pacific Islands and Arab regions of the world. Of these thirty-four countries, twenty-five use a plurality-majority electoral system, and fifteen of those twenty-five are first-past-the-post. Eight of the thirty-four countries either have proportional representation – Liechtenstein, Sri Lanka, Turkey, Algeria and Paraguay – or a semi-proportional electoral system: Armenia, Niger and Jordan.

In summary, of those countries where women are least well represented, one country, the United Arab Emirates, has no direct parliamentary elections at all. Twenty-five countries or 73.5 per cent use a plurality-majority system, and of those more than half use a straight first-past-the-post system. The remaining eight countries, or 23.5 per cent, use some form of proportional representation.

In other words, all the countries with high numbers of women in their legislatures have a PR electoral system, but having a PR system does not automatically translate into a high number of women in the legislature. In fact, a substantial number, almost 25 per cent of those countries with the fewest women, have some form of PR. There must be willingness on the part of political parties to place women's names in positions on voting lists where they can get elected. There must also be willingness on the part of the population at large to vote for the parties that put women's names forward.

In a country where the majority of the population is concerned about gender equality, all political parties will structure their party lists to ensure that women are fairly distributed on the lists, thereby ensuring that adequate numbers are elected from all the parties who elect members. The same, however, will hold true in plurality-majority systems where women can consistently get nominations in winnable seats.

## Challenges and obstacles

In many regions of the world religious or cultural factors may present a significant barrier to the political participation of women. The 1994 Inter-Parliamentary Union Plan of Action identified a long list of necessary precursors to women entering public life. These included not only the obvious religious and cultural values, but also education, health, employment, participation in economic life, as well as the establishment of the legal basis for the equality of men and women. Without addressing these factors, it is clear that the question of the type of electoral system used will not be of great relevance.

Gender inequalities are unevenly distributed in countries throughout the world. Such differences underline the need for approaches that are specific to each country or region of the world. Many developed nations, for example, enjoy equal opportunity in employment and education, but women are still significantly under-represented in public life. This demonstrates that no country should become complacent in the area of gender equity, for the ultimate goal of political, social and economic equality is still a far-off dream everywhere. There is still a need for special measures to rectify the imbalances.

## Corrective measures

Legislation can be a powerful tool to effect change. The issue of affirmative action measures, particularly the use of quotas, has been extremely controversial in many countries, but also very effective. The Nordic counties, with their long history of progressive social policies that provide equality of opportunity, still felt the need to use quotas in order to achieve equality in the political area. As the Speaker of the Swedish Parliament, Birgitta Dahl stated:

> We did not start with a quota system. First we laid the groundwork to facilitate women's entry into politics. We prepared the women to ensure they were competent to enter the field: and we prepared the system, which made it a little less shameful for men to step aside. Then we used quotas as an instrument in segments and institutions where we needed a breakthrough.

According to the Inter-Parliamentary Union data, quotas were used in thirty-four countries by fifty-six political parties in 1992. In addition to quotas, used by either political parties or in legislation, other affirmative action measures such as appointment, twinning, the use of reserved seats, and women-only selection lists have all resulted in significant increases in the numbers of women. In South Africa for example, since the ANC's adoption of a 30 per cent quota, the percentage of women has gone from 2.7 per cent to 29.8 per cent in six years. The IDEA handbook *Women in Parliament: Beyond Numbers* has an extensive section on the use of quotas in both developed and developing countries.

Affirmative action measures are a difficult concept for many people to agree intellectually. They feel that removing formal barriers is all that needs to be done, for with equality of opportunity will come genuine equality. This has not proven to be true. Direct discrimination often exists and unseen barriers also prevent women from entering the political realm and advancing in many countries.

Women need training, mentoring and financial support if they are going to succeed in the political area. EMILY's List has played a critical role in both the United States and in Australia in providing women with the financial assistance needed to succeed.

The organisation began in the United States, helping women in the Democratic Party. EMILY stands for 'Early Money is Like Yeast' – it makes the 'dough' rise. In Australia it has provided women with financial support, training workshops, mentoring, media and campaign support. Since its inception in Australia in 1996 it has established a network of women from all ages and incomes from across the country, and has donated over a quarter of a million dollars to campaigns of women candidates. Its total membership is now over 2000 in Australia and growing, and includes eighty-four of the current 124 Labour women members in Parliament.

As well as financial assistance, training and special education measures are key to addressing the gender imbalance in parliaments. Speaking publicly, voicing opinions, balancing domestic roles with public life are all new roles for most women, and they need encouragement and support. Women must be motivated and encouraged to run. The existing barriers must be overcome before numbers will increase significantly. Social values and cultural traditions need to change, and men must be supportive of the change required. This is not something that women can do alone.

Political parties need to choose women to run in seats that are winnable, and position them on lists where they can get elected. Political parties are in the business of winning elections, and women have proven they can win when given a fair chance. Polls have consistently shown that women are widely perceived as being more honest, hardworking and approachable than men, they are trusted and are electable. Once the major political parties, controlled by men, start to consistently put forward women candidates in significant numbers in winnable seats, gender equality in parliaments can become a reality.

### New Zealand's experience

To return to the question of the significance of the electoral system on the number of women in a legislature, it might be useful to briefly look at the situation in New Zealand, where the country has recently changed from a first-past-the-post plurality system to a mixed-member proportional system. Did this change result in a significant increase in the number of women?

If we look at the data from the last two elections under the first-past-the-post system, in 1990 there were sixteen women elected in a House of ninety-nine, or 16.2 per cent, and in 1993 the number had increased to twenty-one for a total of 21.2 per cent. The first election under the new mixed member proportional system saw only 15.4 per cent elected as constituency members, but 45.5 per cent as list members, for an overall average of 29.2 per cent. The 1999 election saw 23.9 per cent elected as constituency members and 39.6 per cent as list members, for an overall total of 30.8 per cent.

There are definitely more women in the New Zealand Parliament now, and the increase is predominately due to increases in the women members elected from party lists. Clearly, the political parties in New Zealand are now preparing lists of candidates for elections that include substantial numbers of women. Does this mean that the change to a type of proportional representation system is the sole factor responsible for the increase in women? It is unlikely anyone would suggest that is the only reason. It is certainly a factor, in that it is now possible for lists to be structured that favour electing more women, but the willingness of the political parties to ensure favourable placement is an essential requirement as well. In New Zealand the means to elect women is now present, it is coupled with the will to do so, and the numbers are increasing accordingly.

### Choosing the right approach

Are proportional systems necessary for significant numbers of women to get elected? While it is probably true that proportional systems have the greatest potential, they are neither necessary nor sufficient to ensure there will be more women in parliament. Not all proportional systems are equally good at achieving results. Larger lists and larger areas make it easier to have more women included. Closed lists are preferable provided the parties are positioning women fairly on these lists.

Do majority systems discriminate against women? The simple answer is, 'not necessarily'. If political selection procedures provide a level playing field and women are sought out as candidates, encouraged to run and allowed to obtain nominations in winnable seats, they can win elections. The system itself is not the barrier. Women must have access to the resources and training necessary to succeed, and above all societal and cultural attitudes must change to encourage women to run.

How do you work toward changing attitudes? Experience forms attitudes. One of the easiest ways to change attitudes is to start at the grassroots level. Women should be encouraged to build their confidence at that level where they will see that they can get results and succeed. Power and authority need to be shared with women, not just in the political area but across the board, in the civil service, in government, at local levels and in backroom politics. Give women the access and the experience and they will succeed.

Attitude will determine behaviour. Education programmes are important to change social values. Youth parliaments, where boys and girls together can learn democratic values and gain confidence in voicing opinions can be a useful tool for change here.

Women also require access to financial support, political training and mentoring. Political parties must seek out women candidates for winnable seats. Men must be prepared to share power and support women. Clear objectives must be set and specific time frames agreed upon. Only then will equitable numbers of women in the political area become an achievable reality.

# 11 Holding elections: the mechanics

*This section is based upon a paper presented by Mr Ron Gould, Assistant Chief Electoral Officer, Elections Canada, and on the subsequent plenary discussions.*

The process of holding an election has to be country-specific. In other words, it must be designed specifically to work in the country or state where it is to take place. As an example, in the state of Oregon in the United States, at the last presidential election, everyone voted by mail. Every registered voter was sent a ballot two and a half weeks before election day. It was to be filled out and returned by 8 pm on the day of the vote, when it was opened and counted. Such a system would be unlikely to work in many parts of the world because of the potential for fraud. In Oregon it has resulted in higher voter participation and lower costs.

Principally therefore, the mechanics put in place for the holding of the election should take into account things like the democratic maturity and sophistication of the population, literacy levels, complexity of the electoral system, population level and geographic size. Is it to be one simple question or many? Is cost a major factor? Will security be a major problem?

While all issues apply in all countries, the degree will vary enormously. What follows therefore is a brief outline of the basic mechanics required to hold a democratic election.

[ 99 ]

## Fundamentals

### Electoral legislation

An Election Act, which outlines the process, is the only way to ensure that no social group or political party receives any privileges not available to all. Provisions relating to registration of political parties and candidates must be spelled out in the legislation and it must be borne in mind that the ease or difficulty of meeting the requirements set out will directly affect the participation level. The legislation should provide legal protection for all participants, and should specify mechanisms for dealing with complaints, which will ensure impartial and speedy resolution of problems.

### Register of voters

A comprehensive, accurate and up-to-date list of who can vote, and in what area, is essential. The objective is to have a user-friendly process that makes it as easy as possible for everyone who should be on the register to be included. If a register is to be prepared for each election, sufficient lead-time is required to prepare and validate such a register. If a permanent list is maintained, a process needs to be in place to ensure it is kept accurate and up to date, and that regular verifications are made. It needs to be easy to locate a name on the register. There must be a straightforward, credible process in place to challenge, add or delete names. Basic criteria for being on the list must be set down, widely known and adhered to rigorously.

### Political parties and candidates

The fundamental freedoms: freedom of speech, of association, of assembly, of movement, and freedom from fear, all apply to electoral campaigns. The degree to which contributions to political parties and campaign expenditures are regulated will have a major impact on elections. Political parties with more money have an advantage over poorer parties, and a party in power, using government resources during an election campaign, can thereby benefit over others. This needs to be regulated.

As much as possible there needs to be a level playing field so that the election is as fair as possible and is perceived by all to be fair. This also applies to media access.

*Ballots*

The design of the ballot is fundamental to ensuring the integrity of the voting process. The recent US Presidential election has taught us all this fact.

Ballots will differ substantially, depending upon the electoral system, the number of political parties or candidates on the ballot, the number of items to be voted upon, and whether the ballot is paper, mechanical or electronic. The objective in designing the ballot however is common, regardless of the differences in other factors. All ballots must be voter-friendly, be secure and ensure secrecy.

Ballot security, when using paper ballots, may be achieved by using paper with built-in security features such as water marks, micro lettering and so forth. This can however be quite costly. Less expensive and equally if not more effective methods are the use of special poll stamps or initialling by a polling official. Ballots with numbered stubs, which are assigned to specific polls and tracked centrally, are also a very reliable method of preventing fraud.

The ballot design must ensure secrecy. If paper ballots are used, the paper needs to be opaque enough that no one can determine how a person voted through the back. Any numbering of ballots must take place on the stubs, which are removed before the ballot is given to the voter. The numbering is for tracking ballots assigned to specific polls to prevent fraud; it must not allow anyone to determine how someone voted.

The ballot must be as user-friendly as possible. One needs to keep in mind that the lengthier the ballot, the more care needs to be taken in its design. If it is printed on both sides, it must be obvious that it needs to be turned over to complete voting. If more than one page is required, the voter may easily miss a page if numbering is not extremely visible. Using photographs or symbols, in addition to names, enables illiterate voters and those with minor visual impairments to vote without assistance, which saves time and enhances secrecy.

The more complex the ballot, the higher the cost of the election. More needs to be spent in ballot design, in voter education, for printing and distribution costs. The percentage of votes spoiled or incomplete will be higher, and results will be slower to compile. Attention needs to be paid to all these seemingly minor factors, for they all contribute to the success of the process.

*Vote counting*

Counting the vote is an area often dismissed in the design of the election process as being straightforward. Most polls usually have only a few hundred ballots, and counting to 300, either manually or by machine, would not seem to be all that difficult. The problem here lies in the fact that the actual count can be the site of manipulation, fraud, errors and disputes. Only through detailed process design and training for both staff and observers can these possibilities be minimised or eliminated. Things such as tracking and recording the delivery of ballots at the counting centres, and reconciling the number of ballots received with the number of names on the voters list that are marked as having voted, are extremely important in ensuring a fair process.

Decisions must be taken before the election and communicated well in advance of the actual count, as to what constitutes a valid and an invalid ballot. All ballots used in every polling station need to be identical, and the criteria for accepting or rejecting a ballot must be applied uniformly throughout the country. Polling officials, party representatives and observers in all polls need to be trained beforehand to avoid inconsistent interpretations, disputes, and manipulation at the counting stage.

The disputes in Florida in the recent US Presidential election have shown the world that consistency, proper training of staff and transparency in the process are essential to providing credibility to the election results.

*Resolving disputes*

No election, no matter how carefully organised and well run, will be free of disputes, some minor, others potentially extremely serious. It is essential to anticipate this and to have strategies prepared in advance to deal fairly and in a timely manner with any and all complaints.

The courts should be used only as a last resort because the legal process is normally lengthy and expensive and undue delay is likely, which will only exacerbate problems.

*Mechanisms*

The dispute resolution mechanisms, which are designed in advance of the election, need to be easily accessible, affordable and appropriate to the dispute being dealt with. The process must be impartial and be seen to be impartial. It needs to be independent of the government and of all political parties, and able to deal with any and all types of disputes that might arise.

Detailed planning is essential before an election, as to where in the process disputes could arise. Appropriate, independent appeal and review bodies, which have adequate powers and resources, need to be created, with the authority to resolve defined disputes. There need to be local, regional and national bodies, each able to investigate and rule on issues, and an appeal mechanism to a higher level possible, with the courts being the ultimate appeal body. Impartiality and transparency are key in ensuring that the process works fairly and everyone has confidence in it.

*Roles and boundaries*

Electoral boundaries are normally redrawn on a regular basis, for example after a specified period of time, say every ten years, or following a census. An independent electoral boundaries commission can go a long way to ensure that the new boundaries as far as possible do not favour one party or group over another. Adequate consultation and transparency are key here to ensuring fairness and the presumption of fairness.

The electoral roll, no matter how up to date, will always contain names of people who have moved or died, and will also be missing the names of people who have recently moved, just reached voting age or been left off through error. Accessible appeal bodies must be put in place to allow errors to be rectified speedily. The goal to be achieved here is that no qualified voter should be disenfranchised because of errors in the electoral list.

### Parties and candidates

Political party and candidate registration is an area that often gives rise to disputes. Qualifications in order to be registered, the process to be followed, and the date and time requirements for registration, must all be decided well in advance. These decisions must also be well publicised and fairly enforced. Appeal processes need to be impartial, fast and fair. Codes of conduct for parties and candidates, which have been developed through consultation and negotiation, go a long way to minimising conflict.

Access to and use of financial and other resources can be a major source of conflict. Clear regulations or legislation, particularly concerning the use of government resources during an election campaign, are major assets in avoiding problems. A dispute resolution body that is 'politically sensitive' is important for dealing with both party and candidate complaints. The main object here is that all parties are treated as equally and fairly as possible.

### Security and integrity

Events that call into question the security and integrity of the voting process itself must be able to be dealt with both on the spot during the voting or counting, as well as after the election. During the process the presence of representatives from the various parties or candidates, as well as national and international observers, can assist in minimising the number of problems that occur. Adequate procedures are necessary to allow challenges to the process to take place and be dealt with expeditiously and responsibly. Post-election appeals must also have a standardised mechanism in place to deal with them, in which everyone has confidence.

Disputes as to what constitutes a rejected ballot can be minimised with voter education programmes and consistent training of polling staff. The voters need to know beforehand what choices they will be asked to make and how the ballot is to be marked. The staff needs to know what constitutes a valid vote and what does not, and there must be national consistency in those determinations.

Where wrongdoing does occur, the sanctions imposed must be appropriate to the seriousness of the wrongdoing. They can range from fines, payment of compensation, ordering a correction or right of reply in the media, up to suspension or removal of a candidate or party, or imprisonment. Publication of such sanctions in advance can often act as a deterrent.

Dispute resolution mechanisms that are alternatives to the courts include such possibilities as negotiation, mediation, arbitration, commissions of enquiry or fact-finding bodies, negotiated binding rules and so forth. The International Institute for Democracy and Electoral Assistance (International IDEA) is one of several excellent sources for detailed information in this area.

## Conclusion

The ultimate aim of every democracy is to have 'free and fair' elections, where everyone who is entitled to vote is allowed to, free from any threat or fear. The election proceeds without fraud or manipulation, and the decision that results is the will of the majority and accepted by all. The 'free and fair election' is the goal of every democracy. The design and implementation of the proper mechanics for the particular country in question will go a long way to ensuring that goal is met.

# 12 External influences on electoral processes
## i) Exit polls, time zones and length of elections

*The themes for this section are based on a paper by the Hon. Professor Bharati Ray, Ph.D., Member of Parliament – Rajya Sabha – New Delhi, India, and on the associated discussion.*

### Exit polls and time zones

Exit polling is the practice of asking voters as they leave the polling station how they voted. Results are tabulated immediately and the results released. Projections can then be made as to what the results of the election will be, based on the polling results. Do such projections become self-fulfilling prophecies? Exit polling has been criticised in various countries as potentially interfering with election results. Can a strong case be made that it does in fact interfere? What are its real and perceived problems? Should steps be taken to ban or limit exit polling in order to ensure that elections will be fairer?

*Country experiences*

In the United States for example, exit-polling results are often announced within minutes of polls closing. In a country that has only one time zone, that would not be the problem it is in the

United States. When the polls close on the east coast many polls in the west will still be open for several hours. Are voters influenced to change the way they vote based on exit-polling results from other parts of the country? There is thought to be both the 'bandwagon' effect, that is the desire to support the winner, and the 'underdog' effect that wants to shore up the loser. It may indeed influence some people in how they vote.

At present enquiries are being made into whether or not exit polling can be either regulated or perhaps banned entirely in the United States. There is concern however that such regulation may not be possible, for the argument could be made that prohibition of exit polling is against the First Amendment, the guarantee of freedom of speech. In the case of the United States, banning publication by the media until after all polls are closed would do nothing to stop Internet sharing of information. Perhaps alternative measures such as staggering polling hours across the country to try to ensure a uniform closing time might be tried. Even this could prove hard to regulate because the running of elections in the United States is delegated down to the state level and often to the municipal level.

Although Canada also has the problem of six time zones across the country, which means some polls have closed while others are still open, exit polls do not present a problem. This is because in Canada the Elections Act is quite specific about the secrecy of how a person votes. It is illegal to ask people how they voted.

Many countries besides Canada also impose various restrictions on the publication of opinion polls and exit polls. Countries such as France, Italy, Poland, Turkey, Argentina and Colombia all impose some restriction. The most common restriction is to prohibit the disclosure of exit poll results until all polls have closed. Sometimes the prohibition is contained in legislation while in other cases it is constitutional.

In many third world countries where there is genuine fear in having others know how you voted because of the very real danger of reprisals, exit polling could be a serious problem. Restricting the use of such polling through legislation or other means may be a requirement for the protection of voters in such cases.

India has a major problem with respect to exit polls for several reasons. More than 500 million people vote in India across thirty-five states and union territories. Because of the sheer numbers of electors, the large geographic area of the country and the great diversity of languages and cultures, polling for a national election has to be spread over many days.

The elections for the Lok Sabha in 1999 saw polls open in various different regions of the country on 5, 11, 18 and 25 September and 3 October. In some of the very large states, Uttar Pradesh for example, elections were held in different parts of that state on three separate days. Voters in one part of the state would certainly have knowledge through the media of the results of exit polls taken in another part of the state before they voted. This may well have influenced the voting on subsequent days.

There have been heated discussions and numerous articles written in India on the subject of exit polls, and there were legal cases following the 1999 election. There is concern about the publishing of such polls during the election period. There are also questions how reliable the polls are. In some cases, the motives behind the conduct of the polls are questioned. If the polling organisation is politically biased in favour of one political party, might it attempt to influence the outcome of the election by releasing suspect polling results?

Even without intending to skew the results of the exit polls, the interview sample may be too small or unrepresentative. Voters who were canvassed may not be telling the truth, or the results may be wrong or misleading for other reasons.

The media argue they are doing their job of gathering information as best they can and attempting to keep people informed throughout the lengthy election period. Freedom of the press, they argue, is an important democratic right. This argument, however, needs to be balanced against the requirement for fair elections. If the publishing of premature or erroneous exit poll information is hindering the provision of fair elections, then something should be done.

The Election Commission in India had banned the publication of exit polls and opinion polls for the 1999 election. In an order concerning the Dissemination of Opinion Polls dated 20 January 1998 they stated that these polls 'had the potential to influence the electors' and would be 'likely to affect the unbiased exercise of franchise by the elector, one way or the other'.

The Election Commission by Order dated 20 August 1999 prohibited the publication or dissemination in any print or electronic media of any exit poll 'till the closing of poll in all States and Union Territories'. The Commission also required that information concerning the gathering of the data, such as sample size and geographic area, also be included with the results of polls when published.

The Election Commission was taken to court over these rulings. In its judgement the Supreme Court ruled against the Commission, whereupon it withdrew its previous 'Guidelines banning publication and telecast of the results of opinion and exit polls'. The potential problem of exit and opinion polls in India therefore continues.

In Russia the problem of time zones is a significant one. There are eleven different zones and although the election is held during a single day, the polls open at 6 am on one side of the country and close at 11 pm on the other side. Voters are not to be told the results of exit polls until all the polls have closed, but the use of the Internet has begun to be a problem, where polling information is often available to those who look for it. It is quite clear that exit polls affect turnout, particularly in close elections. Whether or not it might change the way people vote is yet to be determined.

*Issues*

What effect exit polls might have on an election will vary widely from country to country and will be dependent upon several factors. First, what is the level of sophistication in the electorate? Is there a high literacy level? Do voters have widespread access to the media? Will large numbers of electors receive the information contained in the exit polls in a timely manner? If most people are unaware of the results obviously the influence level will not be high. The more highly educated and affluent voters are, the more likely they are to become aware of the information. Does that necessarily mean that they will be influenced? In a close election the likelihood of exit poll results encouraging people to get to the polls and vote would certainly be strong, but would it be likely to change their vote? It is not an easy question to answer.

Another significant issue is the reliability of the polls. If the organisations producing the results are consistently poor predictors of the outcomes due to inadequate sampling techniques or deliberate biases in their reporting, people will be apt to disregard the results and not be significantly influenced, one would think. Should this not be the case and voters be swayed by erroneous data, the fairness of the entire process could be at issue. Highly accurate data produced on a consistent basis and distributed rapidly to a literate population are the most likely to potentially affect the results of an election. We are referring here to the undecided or swing voter. Obviously those who always vote the same way will pay little attention one way or the other. The swing vote in most developed countries is growing. Thus, the problem of exit polls is an increasing one.

Countries without restrictions or controls in existence may have to consider introducing legislation or regulations to cope with the problem of exit polls, in order both to protect voters' safety in some areas of the world and to ensure fairness in all elections everywhere. While some may attempt to deal with the problem in other ways, such as altering polling times or enhancing and encouraging the secrecy aspect of a person's vote, this will clearly not be as effective.

### Length of election campaigns

Is the length of the election period a factor in determining the results of an election, and if so, how? The reason for an election campaign is to enable the leadership and the individual candidates of the various political parties to put forward their policies and attempt to persuade the voters to support them. The length of the election period needs to be sufficiently long for those running for election to get their message across, but not so long that the voter is thoroughly tired of the whole process before polling day arrives.

Voters need enough time to decide which leader they like, which candidates they prefer, which policies make the most sense to them and which party they feel is most capable of governing. They need to be able to obtain enough information to make an informed choice between the alternatives offered. How much time that is will be based on a variety of factors, and will vary from country to country.

### Factors to consider

The biggest distinctions with respect to the issue of campaign length are based on the size of the population, the average literacy levels of the voters, the geographic size of the country and the culture and expectations of the voters. Does the population at large have widespread access to electronic and print information, or must campaigning be more hands-on? Cost will also be a great determinant of time requirements. In a large country, travel will be time-consuming and costly. Climate and geography can also be factors. Reaching larger numbers of people will take longer and cost more. All of these factors will interrelate, and determine where and how the majority of the voters obtain the information they need, and how the campaign will be run.

In nearly all cases, the larger, established political parties have a distinct advantage in any election campaign. They can mobilise larger numbers of supporters to work for the party. This includes having campaign workers available to do everything from visiting people in their homes, phoning electors to solicit support, delivering information door to door, manning information booths, and attending rallies and debates to show support.

Larger parties also normally have more money. They can afford to buy better coverage in the media, including television, radio and newspaper advertisements. They have the resources to train and prepare candidates better. They can afford more printed signs and candidate literature. A well organised larger party with adequate resources, both money and people, can just do more and reach more people with their message, better and faster, than a smaller party. The bigger parties are also more able to sustain a campaign over a longer period of time. They will not as easily run out of resources, human or financial.

### Short or long?

A shorter campaign period for an election will therefore marginally assist smaller parties who have less to spend and fewer party workers. It can also reduce the overall cost of the entire campaign significantly. Every day costs money.

A shorter campaign time frame combined with reasonable spending limits imposed by and monitored by an independent electoral authority can help to level the playing field significantly and allow smaller parties a fairer chance of success in elections. The length of the election period can be a major factor influencing the electoral process, and should be considered carefully.

# 12  External influences
# on electoral processes
# ii)  Opinion polling and the
# media

*This section is based upon a presentation given by Professor Robert M. Worcester, Chairman of MORI (Market and Opinion Research International) and of MORI Social Research Institute, London, and on the associated discussions.*

Polling is a part of politics virtually throughout the democratic world. Political parties are constantly testing public opinion on a variety of questions. They want to know what the population thinks about proposed policies, and their opinions of the leadership. The government in power wants a snapshot of how it is doing in the public's view every step of the way. Often it seems that hardly a day goes by when the press is not covering the results of yet another poll on yet another issue.

### Electoral impacts

In countries without fixed election dates, results of polls can play a major part in the choice of when to call an election. No prime minister is likely to decide to hold an election when the governing party is low in the polls, if it can be avoided. In addition, continuous low support from polls on questions of leadership have caused more than one premier or party leader to either decide for him or herself it was time to step down, or to have the decision forced upon him by his or her party.

It has been suggested that polling influences elections in some countries. There has been speculation that in the United States the so-called 'bandwagon' effect of polls means that many people seeing a particular candidate ahead in the polls will be influenced to vote for that person in order to be supporting a winner. While the bandwagon effect has been seen in the United States, that does not necessarily mean that it happens everywhere. The thinking in Great Britain is that the opposite may occur there. People are rallied to support the underdog in the polls, feeling that he or she is not getting a fair shake, or not wanting the winner to receive a landslide.

## The UK situation

In considering the question of the effect polls might have on elections, a crucial factor to consider is just what is the committed level of party support in the country. In the UK for example there are three major political parties, Labour, Conservative and Liberal Democrat. Fully 80 per cent of the population will consistently vote for one of those parties no matter what it does. A committed Labour voter will vote Labour regardless of the changes in policies that the party advocates and no matter who it chooses as leader. This means that the floating vote in the entire country is only about 1.2 million people, or 20 per cent of voters.

In 75 per cent of the constituencies the results never change. The election is always decided in the marginal constituencies, the 25 per cent of ridings that swing back and forth from one party to another and therefore decide the outcome of the election.

Polling in the UK has shown that the governing party's popularity will drop when events transpire that are negative in the public view and will increase when the opposition does something inappropriate. In the 1983 election as an example, when polling during the campaign tested the core vote, 30 per cent supported Labour in spite of an unpopular leader and bad organisation. The core vote for the Tories was 30 per cent and the core vote for other parties was 20 per cent. The floating vote of 20 per cent decided the election.

### Determining factors

For the swing voters, what are the factors that they take into account in coming to their decision? Again here, polling has shown that the decision is based 60 per cent on image and 40 per cent on issues, therefore leadership is the key factor.

In considering the leadership of a party, polling will test support by soliciting information on two main questions. The first one is, do you like him or her? The second one is, do you like his or her policies? Answers to questions on these two basic areas when combined will give the overall leadership rating.

In devising polls, the questions must test those things that can be rated. These are basically five things: behaviour, knowledge, views, attitudes and values. The first three are easy to rate. Attitudes are harder to change, but it is something that can be done through providing more knowledge or by presenting the views of someone the voter respects. Values are very core to a person, and difficult to change.

In testing changes in voter preference during a recent UK election, polling results showed that only 8 per cent changed their voting preference during the actual electoral campaign. Of that total, some 21 per cent said they were influenced by television debates, 15 per cent by newspapers, 10 per cent by the local candidate and 1 per cent by telephone calls. In 1997, 10 per cent of respondents said television was an influence on their voting decision. In 2001, 21 per cent said television was an influence.

Basically people need to think that a party is capable of governing. Their policies on issues are less important than their leadership. Do those in senior positions in the party inspire the voters with the sense of confidence that they could effectively govern the country? Do they like and trust the leader? If the answer is yes, then people will often vote for that party regardless of its stand on various issues. In addition, divided parties do not win elections. That has consistently proven to be true. There must be strong and effective leadership for a party to be elected.

After leadership, the second item of importance to voters in deciding who to cast their vote for relates to current issues. First and foremost the issues being discussed by the candidates during the election period must be important to the voter. Agreeing with the party's policy on an issue is often less important than hearing the candidates raise the issue and treat it as one that must be addressed. The voters want to hear about those topics that they feel are important.

In the most recent election in the UK for example, the Conservative Party consistently talked about Britain's relationship with Europe and the issue of a common currency. Polling, however, showed that the issues of importance to voters at the time, in order of concern, were health care, education, law and order, taxes, Europe, pensions, managing the economy and public transportation. With interest in Europe and a common currency far down the list of voter priorities, it was not surprising that the Conservative Party did not fare well in the election. They simply were not addressing the topics that the voters felt were important.

It is crucial that the issues a party is putting forward during an election campaign are of relevance to the voter. The politicians need to talk about what voters want to hear. For voters to be influenced to support a particular party during an election, they need to hear that party's position on the issues that they feel are important to them. In addition, they must be able to discriminate between the various parties' positions on the issues. Where they feel that all parties are advocating more or less the same thing, there will be little reason to support one party over the other.

The voters must also have confidence that the party expressing concern on an issue that the voters feel is important, will be able to do something to improve the situation on that issue. In addition, they must be persuaded that the party will, if elected, actually attempt to do something about the problem. Issues are extremely important in deciding the vote. Voters need to hear enough about the issues they care about to make up their minds who to support. Only by concentrating on those issues that the voter is concerned about can a party hope to persuade voters to support it in an election.

### The influence of technique

Polling results are dependent upon the skills of those doing the polling. It is a well-known fact that the wording of a question can skew the results, and in some cases may even influence voters. So called 'push polling', which was started in the UK in the 1960s, was designed initially with good intentions. Through interviews, a series of questions were posed which were designed to influence, by means of the wording of the questions. Some groups however have begun to use this method as a means of discrediting, defaming or criticising other parties or candidates. One method of countering such unethical procedures is through the use of professional societies; another is through the courts.

In Australia questions such as, 'Mr. X who advocates paedophilia is a candidate in your constituency. Do you intend to vote for him?' have increasingly been asked during elections. More and more often the courts are being asked to deal with these practices through anti-defamation laws.

The purpose of polling should be to inform, to educate, even to entertain, but it should not be used for anything more than that. Some people advocate the use of polls as an expansion of the democratic process, suggesting that a party in power should canvass the population throughout its mandate on every major issue and act only on majority views. Such a proposal makes little allowance for minority or regional views, and presupposes that all of the population is equally well informed on all issues as the elected member of parliament can be. It also suggests that an opinion poll taken at a particular point in time should carry the decision, even though factors not then widely known or subsequent events may alter views or influence opinions to change. More than anything, it places a great deal of trust in the infallibility of the polling process, something that may not be wise.

## A bottom line

If an elected parliament is to work well, in a democratic way, people have to select the best representatives they can to represent them and then allow these legislators, through debate and informed hearings to come to the best decisions they can on issues. Polling is a wonderful method for those representatives to keep abreast of public opinion on issues. It is, however, only one such method. It should be used as only one additional piece of information in coming to an informed decision – an important piece of information, but not the only one.

# PART IV

---

# COUNTRY-BASED INSIGHTS ON ELECTORAL ISSUES

# 13 Ethnically divided polities: the case of Sri Lanka

*This chapter is based primarily on a discussion led by the Hon. Professor Gamini Lakshman Peiris, Minister of Constitutional Affairs and Industrial Development and Deputy Minister of Finance, Colombo, Sri Lanka.*

Parliament must be reflective of public opinion. If it merely gives lip service to minority participation, a high level of tension in the body politic will result. Sri Lanka has long been known as a place of ethnic conflict. The Tamil problem, which has resulted in a devastating war in the northern and eastern parts of the country, had its roots in the constitutional development of the country.

## Historical context

Before 1931, the United Kingdom had experimented with communal representation whereby particular communities had the possibility of sending representatives to government. This practice was abolished in 1931 when universal adult suffrage was adopted. From 1931 to 1978 the first-past-the-post system was in place.

By 1978 it was realised that a serious representational problem existed. There was little correspondence between the number of votes received and the number of seats obtained. The government in power rode roughshod over minorities and put many institutions in jeopardy.

The Parliament of the day had a mandate for six years. It held a referendum to see if it could continue to govern for another six years and managed thereby to convert a 51 per cent in favour to 49 per cent opposed response into a twelve-year Parliament. There was debate in the country as to how to prevent this from happening again. The legislature during this time had little control over the executive once it became entrenched in power.

In the period from 1931 to 1949 the system did serve minority interests through seven executive committees. The legislature continued to involve itself in the executive through the Parliament, and various ethnic groups were involved.

### Current system

In 1978 it was decided to change to a proportional representation system. The results given by that system have caused a great deal of political instability. It has resulted in very thin majorities. There was an attempt to resolve this by giving a bonus seat to the party with the most seats, one extra seat in each area.

While it was important for constituents to know who their member was and have direct contact, this proved extremely difficult to do when members were elected from a list. It was hard to assign a particular member to any one constituency. It also proved hard to run by-elections, for the next on the list would come into Parliament if a vacancy occurred.

While under first-past-the-post it had been possible to have multi-member constituencies with one candidate chosen to represent each ethnic group, this was no longer possible in the proportional representation system. There was no desire to return to the first-part-the-post system but the existing representational system was nor working either. What were the possible options?

### Suggestions for change

There is now the suggestion of a mixed system, where some of the members would be chosen on a first-past-the-post basis and the rest on a proportional representation basis. The question then is what form of proportional representation should be used. Should it be national or based on districts? Should half the members be elected on a proportional basis and half on first-past-the-post, or should the proportion be higher or lower? What should be done about the representation of minorities? Should there be a form of quota? Angry youths have been a problem in the country. Should a certain number of seats be reserved for those 18 to 35 years of age?

If you choose a proportional representation system, must it apply across the board? It could be argued that the national Parliament should be a hybrid, that is a mix of some candidates elected directly and some through proportional representation, but at the local level first-past-the-post is more important in order to enable the close link between the constituent and the elected member.

What about the problem of minorities located predominantly in certain areas of the country? One option would be to create regional bodies and give them power over significant specified areas. There should be a note of caution here, in that there must be a mechanism for power sharing at the centre. Could this power sharing be achieved in a bicameral legislature? Perhaps the Senate could draw from ethnic minorities. Some feel a second chamber is either superfluous if it has no power, or obnoxious if it has power and uses it for obstruction. To counter these potential problems perhaps the second chamber could be given a specific role such as language issues, conflict resolution or regional matters.

Should all regional governments have the same powers? Giving asymmetrical powers to various regional governments in Sri Lanka makes a great deal of sense, for in some areas there is a demand for power while in others, that is not the case. The Tamil want power in the areas where they predominate. Give it to them. In other parts of the country where it is not wanted at this time, more powers could remain centralised.

How is change being addressed in Sri Lanka? There have been lengthy discussions and dialogue. A Parliamentary Select Committee was formed and discussed the issue of change looking at various options and possibilities. Academics and various groups have been consulted and involved.

## The road ahead

The minorities are afraid of losing their identity and must be protected. Muslims and Hindus have different customs relating to marriage, adoptions and so forth because their religious laws differ. These must be protected. There are different languages that must be taken account of, in dealing with issues relating to schools and public institutions.

The starting point for change must be those things that bind, not those that divide. By building on the commonalities and providing for differences, a workable system will be possible. Unfortunately the Tamil Tigers refused to participate in the discussions. They had little trust in the process and were pursuing independence, unwilling to discuss any alternatives. Many countries have offered support and assistance: India, Bangladesh, the United States, the United Kingdom – the list is very long. In the end however it is really a domestic problem. Perhaps the talented mediator recently offered by Norway will be able to provide the forum that is required.

Sound governance and ethnic security should not be mutually exclusive. It is important to build trust. Many options are possible and with time, patience, compromise and openness, solutions will be found.

The problems in Sri Lanka have shown how important the world community can be. Events such as Commonwealth Parliamentary Association discussion groups and conferences, where information and ideas can be shared, are so important. No problem is ever totally new, and one can always learn from others. While it is never possible to transfer a governmental system directly from one country to another because of cultural and societal differences, it is possible after modifications to benefit from what others have done.

# 14 The United States Presidential election: year 2000

*This section is based upon a presentation by Mr William Pound, Executive Director, National Conference of State Legislatures (NCSL), Denver, United States, and on the associated discussions.*

As people around the world watched the last US Presidential election unfolding in the State of Florida, the question on many people's minds was, 'Could Florida happen elsewhere?' With hindsight, it is now easy to itemise the things that went wrong, and to change practices and procedures in order to ensure that such events will not happen again. It is a useful lesson for others to know what happened and how to avoid similar problems.

### US system

Because the United States has a decentralised election process, state law controls the process and the administration of matters pertaining to federal, state and local elections. In the last election, only eight states had a uniform state-wide system. In most states, Florida included, almost everything devolves to the county level. Each municipality or county designs its own ballot and decides on its own procedures. It is possible, then, to have voters using a multitude of methods to cast their ballot, depending totally upon where they live, and whenever they move, everything could change. There could be machines where the voter pulls a lever to register a vote, or paper ballots, or punchcards, or optical scanning machines or other electronic systems. One state, Oregon, has a state-wide mail-in balloting system.

Voter education and training of poll workers becomes extremely complex, for the process differs widely. Recounts on a large scale, as we all witnessed, become cumbersome and laborious processes where consistency becomes virtually impossible.

## Problems

A joint study by experts from the Massachusetts Institute of Technology and the California Institute of Technology, released in July 2001, found that the problems made public in Florida were only a small part of the total. The study suggests that as many as 6 million votes failed to count nation-wide. It found rates of uncounted ballots in Illinois, Georgia and South Carolina, all higher than Florida. Antique voting machinery, such as the punch card system used in parts of Florida, they suggest, may account for as many as 2 million lost votes across the country.

Americans have to register in order to vote, a process that can require some effort on the electors' part, and can cause various foul-ups. This may have accounted for as many as 3 million lost votes nation-wide. Another million votes were uncounted because of various problems at the voting station, according to the study.

## Reforms underway

What happened in Florida was a wake-up call across the United States, and widespread study and reform began immediately in order to restore public confidence in the election process. In May 2001 Florida passed Bill SB 1118, which contained sweeping election changes. Among the changes, punch card machines are now banned throughout Florida, and all counties are required to purchase electronic or optical scan precinct-count equipment by 2002, for which US$24 million has been voted. A further US$6 million was allocated to voter education, and poll worker recruitment and training. A state-wide voter registration database will be created with US$2 million in funding allocated to that. There will be a uniform ballot designed to be used throughout the state. Uniform recount provisions have been established, and the Secretary of State is developing uniform rules to determine voter intent. There are now uniform standards for voting by overseas citizens, as well as numerous other changes. Florida has clearly moved quickly to restore voter confidence.

Although Florida's election reforms are the most comprehensive to date in the United States, the state is not alone in implementing change. Nearly 1600 bills had been introduced, of which 130 had been signed into law as of 4 May 2001. Some examples of changes introduced include the adoption of new state-wide voting technology for Georgia and Maryland. Virginia has passed a bill requiring state-wide standards for determining what constitutes a valid ballot. Washington has approved state-wide procedures for recounts.

The Motor Voter Act has made it far easier and more convenient for voters to register, which could add millions of new voters at the next election. It will also make the job of maintaining accurate voter lists more complicated. By May 2001, Indiana, Colorado and Florida had passed bills to create state-wide voter registration lists, and a number of other states had either begun or upgraded state-wide registration databases.

Several states have passed legislation to prevent fraud at elections. Registering and voting more than once is now a crime in Virginia, and in Vermont is now subject to higher penalties. Tampering with voting equipment in Georgia is now a felony.

Voter education is a subject that has been given widespread attention. Among the many ideas being explored here are state-wide standards for voter education, better instructions on ballots and in polling places, mailing information pamphlets to all registered voters, better education in civics in the schools, and conducting a campaign to teach voters how to use their new voting systems before the next Presidential election in 2004.

## Possible further steps

The very close election results in the United States have served to raise awareness of weaknesses in numerous aspects of the election system throughout the country. To fix the system, voter registration must be improved; voter education is required; poll workers need better training; uniform standards are required for counts and recounts; fraud and intimidation need to be attacked.

In the larger picture, the cost of running for office in the United States is getting to the point where only the very wealthy can put their names forward. It has been estimated that to get elected to the Senate, it is necessary to raise US$10–15 000 each day.

Should there be government funding of election campaigns in order to make it more democratic? Would full public disclosure of all political and campaign funding not go a long way to solving problems? Should limits for election spending be looked at again? There are still many areas of reform that need to be debated and considered before the United States electoral system is as democratic as most people would wish it to be.

# 15 Disputed election results: various African experiences

*This section is based upon a presentation by the Hon. Priscilla Misi-hairabwi, Member, Movement for Democratic Change, Parliament, Harare, Zimbabwe, and on the corresponding discussions.*

In the early years of political independence in many African states, either legislated or de facto one-party rule was the norm. The evolution into multi-party democracies has varied widely from country to country, progressing peacefully in some areas, while in others violence and political struggle has ensued.

### Recent experiences

Between 1990 and 2000, governments in Sao Tome, Cape Verde, Benin, Zambia and Ghana all changed as a result of elections, not civil wars, *coups d'état* or controlled successions. The contesting candidates accepted the outcomes of the elections, as did their parties, and peaceful transitions of power occurred.

The December 1980 elections in Uganda, however, were followed by a civil war. It was alleged the election itself was marred by acts of violence. Allegations of intimidation, fraud and vote manipulation were also made. An armed struggle, lasting some six years, ensued before Milton Obote was overthrown.

In Zimbabwe, the June 2000 election has resulted in numerous candidates and political parties contesting the results in various constituencies. There were allegations of violence and intimida-tion. Many results were contested in courts of law. In some recounts, the results have stood, while in others by-elections were required to be held. In contesting the election results, arguments have included everything from acts of violence and intimidation before and during the election, to fraud and manipulation in ballot counting, to irregularities in voter registration and the conduct of the campaign.

The success of many of the post-colonial elections, for example Zimbabwe in 1980, was credited to the presence of international observers. However the same did not hold true for post-independence elections. African governments, like those of all countries, are protective of their sovereignty and respectful of the principle of non-intervention. The presence of international monitors was viewed with considerable scepticism in many cases.

### A possible solution

Elections require public confidence to be successful. What can be done to restore confidence in the fairness and efficacy of the electoral process, in order to legitimise the outcome? It is suggested that domestic monitors could play a significant role in the entire election process.

Non-partisan domestic observers could be selected from broad-based respected groups that have significant credibility such as religious leaders, human rights organisations, law societies or institutions of higher learning. Their presence at polling stations could deter many forms of intimidation, and provide voters with a sense of security. Because they are familiar with the country's languages, culture and political situation, they could work with international monitoring teams, providing pre-election briefings and advice.

International observers would continue to play a crucial role in reassuring the local population about the efficacy of the electoral process, the secrecy of the ballot and the safety of voters. Their presence needs to be well publicised and accepted by the contesting parties. The international observers also help to deter fraud and manipulation in the balloting and counting process, and can report to the international community about the overall fairness of the election process.

Effective, non-partisan, domestic observer teams, working alongside well-briefed international monitors, would complement each other and greatly increase the likelihood of free and fair elections taking place.

# 16 Evolving electoral systems: the experience of Poland

*This section is based upon a presentation by Professor Jerzy Jaskiernia, Member of the Sejm (Parliament), Poland, and on the associated workshop and plenary session discussions.*

The year 1989 presented the countries of Central Europe with enormous choices and opportunities with regard to systems of government. The new political situation allowed those countries emerging from a totalitarian past to choose both their form of democratic government and the type of electoral system that would be used to select their legislatures.

The population at large was generally familiar with the various political systems existing throughout the world and how they worked. Political science professors and constitutional law experts in these countries possessed detailed theoretical knowledge of the various possibilities. While the theoretical knowledge of various systems and how they worked was universally good, the practical experience of the majority was based solely on single party government. The political elites were now faced with deciding which system would best serve the expectations of the population at large and would create the type of government they wanted. The method of choosing the make-up of the legislatures was going to be intrinsic to how the government would operate.

## Fundamental choices

The fundamental choice was between a majority-type system such as the United Kingdom or the American models, and a proportional system such as exists in Italy and Spain. The mixed-type system in Germany was also one that many found attractive.

If the leaning was toward a proportional system, the question then was what kind of proportional system it should be: one that favoured fewer large parties or one that would result in more and smaller parties? This very important decision also required consideration of the question whether or not thresholds should be imposed for the proportional distribution.

If an analysis was undertaken of the discussions that took place at the time and the different types of electoral laws that were subsequently put into place in the various Central European countries, it would be found that the decisions taken followed from the answer to the following question: which system best provides a suitable mix between fair representation of the majority of the political forces in the country and, at the same time, the likelihood of creating stable, workable government? There is no question that the choice of an electoral system directly influences both the shape of the political system and the possibility of creating a stable government.

## Polish experience

Poland provides an interesting case study of how choices were made and how change has evolved since the initial decisions were taken. By a 'round table agreement' in 1989, it was decided that the Senate, or upper house in Poland, would be elected on a majority system basis. Every region of the country – at that time there were forty-nine – would have two seats. This was based on the model of the United States Senate, with two senators per state. There would be two exceptions, Warsaw and Katowice, which two major regions would each have three seats. Each party was entitled to present only two (or three) candidates in each region. In all regions, the two (or three) candidates with the most votes would be elected senators.

This system was amended slightly in 2001. Because Poland has sixteen provinces, the 100 Senate seats were distributed across the provinces, with either two or three seats to every district. The system of electing these Senate seats remained identical to what it had been. This new system of Senate seat distribution has eliminated a major criticism of the previous system. Because Poland is not a federal state, it had been argued that it was unfair for unequal provinces to have equal representation. The seats are now distributed among the parliamentary districts on the basis of proportional representation.

The system of election to the Sejm, the powerful lower house, is far more complicated. It was decided that it would be impossible to use a majority system for this house because of the very diverse political spectrum in the country. There were initially more than 250 registered political parties.

A majority system would have run the risk of segmenting the parliament to such an extent that it would have been impossible to form a stable government. Either that situation would have occurred, or large portions of society would have received no representation at all, which would have created frustration and led to alienation.

Political theorists have suggested that Poland may in the future change to the majority model, when the political scene has stabilised and the number of major political parties running for parliament is reduced to a small number.

The 1991 election was run on a proportional representation system (the Sainte-Legue system). The results were that the largest number of seats held by any one party was sixty-two, this was of the total 460 seats in the Sejm. In all, seventeen parties had elected members. A government was eventually put together composed of seven parties, and they governed until losing a vote of non-confidence in 1993, whereupon the President dissolved parliament and new elections were held.

Because there was widespread criticism of the fragmented situation created by the 1991 election, one of the immediate steps taken by the newly elected government in 1991 was to change the electoral law. A 5 per cent threshold was introduced in order for political parties to be included in the division of seats following an election. This was to take effect with the next election.

The 1993 election, carried out using a proportional representation system (the d'Hondt system) with a 5 per cent threshold, resulted in six parties electing members. A two-party government (left-centre) was formed and survived the entire term. The problem was that several right-wing parties had not reached the five per cent threshold. As a result some 30 per cent of the votes from that election was not represented in the Sejm.

The 1997 elections were held with no change in the rules. Six parties qualified and a two-party right of centre government with a clear majority was formed. Due to disputes among the coalition partners, it did not survive a full term.

In 2001 parliament again changed the electoral law, this time back to the Sainte Legue proportional system, but with a 5 per cent threshold. Pre-election polling had suggested there was large support for the left, some 43 per cent, while other parties were not showing support higher than 17 per cent. The argument was that parliament should properly express the diversity of the country, and the change would favour smaller parties, which it was argued would better reflect the division in society.

The government has, since this most recent change in the electoral law, been criticised for altering the law so close to an election. It was felt by many not to be fair to have a situation where the majority in power can change the election law to potentially benefit its own interests. It has been recommended that, in the future, such changes should be waiting 'on the shelf' until after the election, to enable the new parliament to make such a decision, which would not then be seen to potentially benefit the current incumbents of the legislature.

### Lessons learned

Over the period of the past six elections in Poland, there have been changes to the electoral system three times. Although there remains a firm conviction that the majority prefers a proportional representation system, the question is still, 'What kind?' Should there be many smaller parties or fewer larger ones?

In the first election there were some 250 registered parties, and some feared the potential lack of a stable government. A threshold of 5 per cent was then imposed for the second election, whereby any party that did not receive 5 per cent of the vote was not included in the distribution of seats. The intent here was to reduce the number of parties to a manageable level. The trade-off in reducing the potential total of parties elected was that some 30 per cent of the vote in the 1993 election did not translate into seats elected. Recently, in 2001, the system was changed yet again.

There is obviously no easy way to select what best suits a country when you begin from scratch. What best suits the people? What system is the best fit with the previous experience of the population? In finding the right balance between stable government and adequate representation it is important not to deter people from participating. After all, democracy is all about participation, having a say in how you are governed.

There needs to be enough room for all voices to be heard, but at the national level in particular, a strong cohesive government is also an important consideration. The men and women chosen to represent the people have to be in a position to get on with the job and run the country. Finding just the right mix where both are possible will take some time and experimentation, both for Poland and elsewhere.

There would appear to be a tendency among newer democracies to concentrate on being representative. Particularly when emerging from a military dictatorship or a regime of tyranny, people seem to both want and need to participate fully. In a context such as Poland's transition to democracy, there needs to be room in a new system for, say, the 'Beer Lovers Party'. It is important that the populace recognise that political parties do not all have to be composed exclusively of serious, blue-suited, middle-aged men. Rather, it is important to demonstrate that diversity makes democracy strong and vibrant.

Older, more mature democracies seem to concentrate more on good governance and stability. Often this can be at the expense of inclusion and compromise. Often they will struggle with low voter turnout at election time, voter apathy and cynicism. The criticism is often heard that all parties offer the same thing, that there is no choice.

## A balanced perspective

No country can expect to have it absolutely right all the time. Continuous discussion and fine-tuning of the system are the only ways to ensure that the delicate balance between participation and inclusion on the one hand, and stability and good governance on the other, is maintained.

Watching the evolution of democratic government in countries like Poland is an extremely useful exercise. Others can learn from the adjustments that are being made to the electoral system in Poland in an attempt to provide a fair balance between the conflicting goals of providing for adequate representation of all political views in the country, and providing the means to consistently elect a stable parliament.

Analysing the results achieved in Poland and the other emerging European democracies is useful for all other countries in the world, in considering their options for change. Ultimately however, each country must determine for itself which approach to democracy will work best for it.

# 17  The New Zealand experience of changing electoral systems

*This section is based upon a presentation by Ms Janet Mackey, Member of Parliament, Wellington, New Zealand, and on the associated discussion in workshop and in plenary.*

New Zealand is a country that is currently being followed closely by those with particular interest in electoral systems, for it has recently changed from a first-past the-post system to a proportional system.

Why did it change? There was probably no one reason. For many years power had alternated between the Labour Party and the National Party. With most seats in the country safe for one party or the other, elections were decided in a handful of marginal seats. Many voters in safe seats felt there was little point in voting at all, for it hardly seemed to matter.

### Historical context

New Zealand abolished its upper house in 1951. There were those who felt the lack of a second chamber was a strong reason that their unicameral Parliament should be made more representational. Some wanted a way to ensure fairer representation for Maori, for women, and for minor parties who had at times received significant voter support but few seats. As an example, the Social Credit gained 20.7 per cent of the popular vote in the 1981 election but this gave the party only two seats in a legislature of ninety-nine seats. The New Zealand Party in 1984 received 12.3 per cent of the vote but not a single seat. Some people simply felt any change would be acceptable because there was widespread dissatisfaction with the status quo.

In 1985, a Royal Commission on Electoral Reform was set up, as a response to public concern. It looked at all options and produced a comprehensive and thorough report, which suggested that the existing system had serious deficiencies. It unanimously recommended change. Subsequently, the government held a referendum asking whether there was a desire for change to the voting system and, if so, which of four options was preferred. The preference was 84.7 per cent in favour of change, and 70.5 per cent in favour of the German model of a mixed-member proportional system (MMP).

A second binding referendum was then held at the next election in 1993, asking voters to choose between the status quo first-past-the-post system (FPTP) and the preferred model of MMP. The question was decided by a vote of 54 per cent to 46 per cent in favour of introducing MMP. Major constitutional change was therefore to be introduced with the 1996 election, based on a very narrow majority vote.

### A new system

The new system increased the number of seats in the legislature from 99 to 120. Each voter was to have two votes, one for a constituency member and one for a political party. Just over half the seats were to be for members to represent the various constituencies, and these were to be selected on the first-past-the-post basis. For the remaining seats, the voter would choose the political party of preference from national lists of candidates. The votes for parties would produce national totals. Candidates from the party lists were then to be allocated seats in the legislature in addition to those elected from the same party to represent constituencies, in order that the total would reflect the overall percentage of votes cast. A party needed to win either one constituency seat or 5 per cent of the total vote to be included in the distribution.

The proportional seats selected from the lists are allocated in the order in which the names appear on the party lists. A candidate may run in an electoral district and also be on the party list. If elected to a district, the individual is then passed over on the list when seats are allocated from there. For example, if a party obtains 50 per cent of the votes cast for party lists it is entitled to half of the 120 seats. If it has elected forty-five members for constituencies, it also obtains fifteen members from its party list, in order to bring its overall total to 50 per cent.

With the decision made and the new system decided upon, the transition period began. The period from 1993 to the first election under MMP in 1996 was one of considerable turmoil. The Standing Orders of the Parliament were revised to fully recognise political parties by, for example, allocating time in debate and membership on committees on the basis of party strength. The public service undertook a review of how it would operate under multiparty government. The Governor General publicly clarified his role with respect to the formation of a government.

Electoral boundaries had to be redrawn completely, significantly increasing the size of constituencies. Political parties needed to establish selection procedures for MMPs. How were the party lists to be drawn up? The reduction in constituency seats from ninety-nine under FPTP to just over half of 120 under MMP meant many incumbents were fighting each other for nominations to constituencies and for their order of placement on the party list. Parties had to consider a multitude of factors in ordering their lists, because obviously the lower down the list a name was placed, the less chance that person had of being elected. Parties also had to consider factors such as gender, geography, ethnicity and ability to win.

Because of the scramble from sitting members for nominations and placements on the lists, and the resulting widespread infighting within parties, coupled with the enhanced possibilities for smaller parties to get elected under MMP, there were widespread party defections. The existing government which had only had a one-seat majority in the 1993 election was reduced first to a majority coalition, then to a minority coalition, then to a single party minority, back to a majority coalition, and finally to another minority coalition in the lead-up to the election.

### Election outcomes

Finally in October 1996 the first MMP election was held. There were twenty-one registered parties of which six managed to elect members. However, no one party had a majority of seats. The turnout at the polls was extremely high at 88.2 per cent. The public was then required to wait over two months while negotiations between the various parties took place behind closed doors as to who would form the government. The first coalition lasted from December 1996 to August 1998. The National Party then continued in power with the support of several newly independent MPs. Those party defections caused serious political and public resentment.

The 1999 election saw twenty-two parties contesting, with seven successful in electing members. Voter turnout was reduced to 84.8 per cent, the lowest since the mid-1970s. Again, no party won a clear majority but a loose coalition was formed fairly quickly and assumed power.

There is currently serious consideration being given to legislation that will prevent sitting MPs from changing parties without giving up their seats. There is also discussion of reverting to the previous FPTP system versus continuing with the present MMP system. Some polling has shown a consistent preference for FPTP over MMP since 1996.

### Lessons and issues

What are the lessons to be learned from the New Zealand experience? First and foremost, there is no perfect electoral system. They all require trade-offs, and people should be aware of those trade-offs before embarking on change. Clearly the degree of instability that the change in the electoral system caused in New Zealand was not recognised in advance or anticipated. The question of party-hopping is one that should probably be discussed and decided upon in advance of an electoral system change. There should be a significant education process in advance of asking the public to decide upon alternative electoral systems, because the options are many and not easy to either explain or understand. What works well in one country may not necessarily work the same way in another. Careful thought and discussion is clearly required before such significant decisions are taken.

There are now two types of members in the New Zealand House of Representatives. Those who represent constituencies have seen them virtually double in size, both geographically and in number of voters since the change. They complain of enormously increased workloads, while those MPs from the party lists have virtually no constituency work. The public, who were accustomed to knowing their member, are now much distanced from their constituency representative because of the increased size, and they have little contact with or knowledge of the list members.

Complaints have been raised that it is now impossible to get rid of an unpopular MP, for even when defeated in a constituency election, if placed high enough up on the party list he or she is elected anyway. It is argued that there is therefore less accountability.

Changing an electoral system is going to impact upon all the other components of the existing governance system of a country, and the transition period will likely be a difficult one for all, both the political parties, the MPs, the other components of the governance system, the accountability structures and the public at large. This needs to be understood and allowed for.

In the previous FPTP system in New Zealand, a small percentage of the population, basically those in marginal seats, decided who would govern. Now under MMP, while the electorate has the power to determine the size and number of political parties elected, who is to form the government has been and will likely continue to be determined by negotiations held in secret by the elected parties. Minor parties or independents will often hold the balance of power.

On the plus side of the change in New Zealand, there is little doubt that Parliament is now more representative of the country as a whole. As in any PR system, all votes now count. As one MP stated:

> Parliament is no longer composed almost solely of dark-suited middle-aged men. There are women, there is a Chinese list MP, there are Pacific Islanders, Maori are not represented only through the Maori constituencies, and we have dreadlocks and a transvestite.

There are more minority parties and single-issue parties. More back-room negotiations are required to get legislation passed. Of necessity there is more consultation and compromise. The government of the day no longer has the power to force extreme or unpopular change.

### The botton line

Many voted for MMP to make the House of Representatives a better place. To what extent have they succeeded? It is probably too soon to say. As with any significant change, it takes times to adjust to the new way of operating and for fine-tuning and adjustments to be made. It must also be borne in mind that no one change is going to rectify instantly all previous problems. As a bottom line, it must be remembered that any parliament, no matter how it is chosen, is composed of politicians, and is as good as the men and women who make it up.

# Afterword

Continuing the dialogue and discussion on the issues of democracy, parliament and electoral systems is crucial to keeping democratic governance functioning well. No one has the perfect system for every population's needs and aspirations. No one has all the answers for all times and places. No system or practice will be universal. Diversity must be accommodated and systems adapted to allow for differences. Democratic government will only function well when there is continuous scrutiny and adjustment.

Gatherings such as the one jointly sponsored by the Commonwealth Parliamentary Association and Wilton Park at Wiston House in June 2001 provide vitally important focal points for elected members, parliamentary officials, scholars and academics, experts and observers to gather together to share knowledge, discuss problems and explore ideas. All participants left that session richer in understanding than when they arrived, and took back home with them additional insights. While all the questions did not find complete answers, much was learned, and the knowledge gained has been carried back to the over thirty countries that were represented.

The dialogue must continue, and hopefully the foregoing distillation of the ideas exchanged at Wiston House will contribute to sustaining it.

# APPENDICES

# Appendix A

## Democracy, Parliament and Electoral Systems: A Commonwealth Parliamentary Association/Wilton Park Conference, 11–15 June 2001

## List of participants

AGUIRRE GIL DE BIEDMA, Esperanza
**Spain**
Speaker, Senate

AL-KAMYANI, Salim
**Oman**
Vice-President Msjlid Ash-Shura

ANANIEVA, Elena
**Russia**
Senior Researcher, Diplomatic Academy, Ministry of Foreign Affairs

BANGURA, Zainab Hawa
**Sierra Leone**
National Co-ordinator, Campaign for Good Governance

| | |
|---|---|
| CARR, Gary | **Canada** |
| | Speaker, Legislative Assembly |
| | of Ontario |
| CARTWRIGHT, Timothy | **Council of Europe** |
| | Head, Planning and Evaluation |
| | Department, Directorate of |
| | Strategic Planning, Council of |
| | Europe, Strasbourg |
| CHUCK, Delroy | **Jamaica** |
| | Spokesman on Justice, Jamaica |
| | Labour Party |
| CLARK, Lesley | **Australia** |
| | Parliamentary Secretary to the |
| | Premier and Minister for Trade, |
| | Queensland |
| COPE, David | **United Kingdom** |
| | Director, Parliamentary Office of |
| | Science and Technology, |
| | Houses of Parliament |
| DIPLOCK, Shelagh | **United Kingdom** |
| | Director, Hansard Society |
| DONAHOE, Arthur | **Commonwealth Parliamentary** |
| | **Association** |
| | Secretary-General, Commonwealth |
| | Parliamentary Association |
| FLEISCHER, David | **Brazil** |
| | Full Professor & Graduate |
| | Coordinator, University of Brasilia |
| FONSEKA, Jennifer | **Commonwealth Parliamentary** |
| | **Association** |
| | Secretary, Development and |
| | Planning, Commonwealth |
| | Parliamentary Association |
| | Secretariat |
| FUSITU'A, 'Eseta | **Tonga** |
| | Deputy Chief Secretary and |

| | |
|---|---|
| | Secretary to the Cabinet, Prime Minister's Office |
| GEORGES, Elton | **British Virgin Islands**<br>Deputy Governor, Government of the British Virgin Islands |
| GHAZI BIN RAMLI, Dato'Hasbullah | **Malaysia**<br>Senator, Parliament of Malaysia |
| GOULD, Ronald | **Canada**<br>Assistant Chief Electoral Officer, International Services, Elections Canada |
| GRIFFITH-TRAVERSY, Mary Anne | **Commonwealth Parliamentary Association**<br>Former Deputy Clerk, Canadian House of Commons |
| GUNDA, Patrick | **Botswana**<br>Legal Officer, Independent Electoral Commission |
| HARRIS, Dame Bridget | **Antigua**<br>Speaker, Parliament of Antigua and Barbuda |
| HASSAN, Feroz | **Bangladesh**<br>Secretary-General, Fair Election Monitoring Alliance (FEMA) |
| HO, Pui-ling Doris | **Hong Kong**<br>Principal Assistant Secretary, Constitutional Affairs Bureau, Government Secretariat |
| HOPKINSON, Nicholas | **United Kingdom**<br>Deputy Director, Wilton Park |
| JASKIERNIA, Jerzy | **Poland**<br>Member of Parliament, Sejm |
| JOHNSSON, Anders | **Inter-Parliamentary Union**<br>Secretary-General, Inter-Parliamentary Union |
| JOSEPH, Lloyd | **Guyana** |

|  | Attorney at Law |
| KHAN, Moyeen | **Bangladesh** |
|  | Member of Parliament |
| KONJORE, Willem | **Namibia** |
|  | Deputy Speaker, National Assembly |
| KWARI, Suleiman | **Nigeria** |
|  | Member, Federal House of Representatives |
| LEE, Sandy | **Canada** |
|  | Member of the Legislative Assembly of the Northwest Territories, Yellowknife |
| LI, Wing | **Hong Kong** |
|  | Chief Electoral Officer, Registration and Electoral Office |
| LIKATE, Mokhele | **Lesotho** |
|  | Commissioner, Independent Electoral Commission |
| MACKEY, Janet | **New Zealand** |
|  | Member of Parliament |
| MADDOCK, Baroness Diana | **United Kingdom** |
|  | Officer, All-Party Group on Electoral Reform, House of Lords |
| MAIA, Ana | **Canada** |
|  | Senior English Speechwriter, Department of National Defence |
| MANGAL, Keshav | **Guyana** |
|  | Medical practitioner |
| MANNING, Patrick, Hon. | **Trinidad and Tobago** |
|  | Leader of the Opposition |
| MISIHAIRABWI, Priscilla | **Zimbabwe** |
|  | Member of Parliament |
| MOHAMMED, Sibongile | **Swaziland** |
|  | Deputy Head, Secretariat, Constitutional Review Commission and Elections Office |

NEHOYA, Immanuel — **Namibia**
Acting Principal Parliamentary
Clerk, National Assembly

NORTON, Professor Philip — **United Kingdom**
Professor of Government,
University of Hull

OKOYE, Festus — **Nigeria**
Vice-Chair, Transition Monitoring
Group, Kaduna

PALAI, Mothusi — **Botswana**
Deputy Permanent Secretary
(Political Affairs),
Office of the President

PALASCIO, Myrtle — **Belize**
Chief Elections Officer, Elections and
Boundaries Department, Ministry of
Public Service

PEIRIS, Gamini Lakshman — **Sri Lanka**
Minister of Constitutional Affairs
and Industrial Development;
Deputy Minister of Finance

POPE, Jeremy — **United Kingdom**
Director, Transparency International

POUND, William — **United States of America**
Executive Director, National
Conference of State Legislatures
(NCSL)

PRESTON, John — **United Kingdom**
Tutor and postgraduate student,
London South Bank University

RAHMAN, Irfan — **Mauritius**
Electoral Commissioner, Electoral
Commissioner's Office

RALITSIE, Khothatso — **Lesotho**
Director of Elections, Independent
Electoral Commission

| | |
|---|---|
| Ray, Bharati | **India** |
| | Member of Parliament, Rajya Sabha |
| Ray, Robert | **Australia** |
| | Senator for Victoria, Parliament of Australia |
| Robertson, Erin | **United Kingdom** |
| | Press and Public Affairs Officer, British Consulate-General, Los Angeles |
| Ryan, Selwyn | **Trinidad and Tobago** |
| | Head, Institute of Economic and Social Research, University of the West Indies, St Augustine |
| Saboor, Abdul | **Pakistan** |
| | Legal Adviser, Pakistan International Human Rights Organization |
| Savill, Margaret | **United Kingdom** |
| | Policy Desk, Commonwealth Co-ordination Department, Foreign and Commonwealth Office |
| Seeletso, Tiro | **South Africa** |
| | Secretary, Independent Electoral Commission |
| Staddon, Anthony | **Commonwealth Parliamentary Association** |
| | Assistant Director, Development and Planning, Commonwealth Parliamentary Association Secretariat |
| Syed, M | **Bangladesh** |
| | Chief Election Commissioner, Bangladesh Election Commission |
| Tripathi, Hon. Keshari Nath | **India** |
| | Speaker, State Legislative Assembly, Uttar Pradesh |
| Webb, Paul | **United Kingdom** |

|  | Professor of Politics, Sussex University |
| Woo, Kwok Hing | **Hong Kong** <br> Chairman, Electoral Affairs Commission |
| Worcester, Robert M. | **United Kingdom** <br> Governor and Visiting Professor of Government at the London School of Economics and Political Science (LSE); Director, Going for Green; Chairman, Market & Opinion Research International (MORI) |
| Zaki, Muhammad Akram | **Pakistan** <br> Senator, Senate of Pakistan |

# Appendix B

## Reference material

The following list of background material does not attempt in any way to be a complete bibliography on the entire book. It covers only websites that readers may not be familiar with, that provide access to additional information on many of the topics covered. It also lists various articles, journals and texts that were either referred to by conference participants or that I found useful when preparing the book.

### Websites

**Commonwealth Parliamentary Association (CPA)**
http://www.comparlhq.org.uk

The CPA has information about the CPA and its activities, upcoming conferences and seminars, as well as material about Commonwealth countries, special reports and statistics.

**Inter-Parliamentary Union (IPU)**
http://www.ipu.org

The IPU has an extensive website with information about the IPU and its activities and data, statistics, publications and bibliographies on world parliaments, as well as links

to various other relevant sources and databases. For statistics and information on women in parliaments see in particular:
'Women in Parliaments':
http://www.ipu.org/wmn-e/classif.htm
'Women in Politics':
http://www.ipu.org/iss-e/women.htm

## National Council of State Legislatures (NCSL), United States
http://www.ncsl.org

For information on electoral reform currently underway in the USA and on the NCSL Special Task Force on Election Reform see:
http://www.ncls.org/programs/legman/elect/taskfc

## Transparency International
http://www.transparency.org

See in particular Transparency International Source Book 2000: 'Confronting Corruption – The Elements of a National Integrity System':
www.transparency.org/sourcebook

## United Nations sanctioned and developed ACE Project (Administration and Cost of Elections)
http://www.aceproject.org

This site has information on electoral legislation and systems, voter registration, vote counting and so forth, also examples from various countries throughout the world

## Wilton Park
http://www.wiltonpark.org.uk

This is the Wilton Park website that provides details about conference programmes, reports, publications, latest news and so forth.

## Articles and texts

International Institute for Democracy and Electoral Assistance (International IDEA), Stockholm:

*The Future of International Electoral Observation: Lessons Learned and Recommendations.*

Reynolds, A. and Reilly, B. (1997) *The International IDEA Handbook of Electoral System Design.*

*Women in Parliament: Beyond Numbers*, handbook (1998).

Beck, J. Murray (1957) *The Government of Nova Scotia*, University of Toronto Press, Toronto.

Brassard, Daniel *How Can Information Technology Transform the Way Parliament Works?* Library of Parliament, Canada, Parliamentary Research Branch.

California Institute of Technology and Massachusetts Institute of Technology (2000) *Voting: What Is and What Could Be*, CIT/MIT Joint Voting Technology Project (available on http://web.mit.edu/voting/).

Drage, Jennifer (2001) 'From the ballot box to the mailbox', *State Legislatures* (Jul/Aug).

Hopkinson, Nicholas (2001) *Parliamentary Democracy: Is There a Perfect Model?* Commonwealth Parliamentary Association, Ashgate Publishing, England.

Institute for Research on Public Policy (IRPP) (2001) 'Votes and seats', *Policy Options*, Vol. 22, No. 6 (Jul/Aug), IRPP, Montreal.

Lougheed, Peter (2001) 'More free votes will lead to more responsible government', *Public Policy Forum*, Vol. 2, No. 2 (Summer).

Milner, Henry (2001) 'Civic literacy in comparative context', IRPP, Montreal.

Norton, Philip (Lord Norton of Louth) (2000) *Norton Report: The*

*Report of the Commission to Strengthen Parliament* (available on http://www.charter88.org.uk/pubs/brief/0007norton.html).
Storey, Tim (2001) 'Putting chads to rest', *State Legislatures* (Jul/Aug).